Brigid Keenan is an author and journalist. Now Fashion Editor at the *Oldie*, she has worked as an editor on *Nova* magazine, the *Observer* and the *Sunday Times*. Brigid is a founding board member of the Palestine Festival of Literature. She has spent most of her life in far-flung diplomatic postings, but now lives with her husband in Pimlico and Somerset; they have two daughters and four grandchildren.

# FULL MARKS FOR TRYING

From her early beginnings — a colourful childhood in India brought to an abrupt end by independence and partition, a return to dreary post-war England, and on to a finishing school in Paris — Brigid Keenan was never destined to lead a normal life. When, as a ten-year-old, she overheard herself described as 'desperately plain', she decided to rely on something different: glamour, eccentricity, character, a career — anything so as not to end up at the bottom of the pile. And in classic Brigid style, she somehow ended up with them all. In the swinging sixties, she came into her own: working with David Bailey and Jean Shrimpton; labelled a 'Young Meteor' by the press; turning up to report on the Vietnam War in a miniskirt . . .

BRIGID KEENAN

# FULL MARKS FOR TRYING

An unlikely journey from the Raj
to the rag trade

*Complete and Unabridged*

# CHARNWOOD
*Leicester*

First published in Great Britain in 2016 by
Bloomsbury
London

First Charnwood Edition
published 2017
by arrangement with
Bloomsbury Publishing Plc
London

The extract on p. 129 is taken from 'How to Get On
in Society', from *Collected Poems* by John Betjeman
© 1955, 1958, 1962, 1964, 1968, 1970, 1979, 1981,
1982, 2001. Reproduced by permission of John
Murray Press, an imprint of Hodder and Stoughton.

*A catalogue record for this book is available
from the British Library.*

ISBN 978–1–4448–3174–0

Published by
F. A. Thorpe (Publishing)
Anstey, Leicestershire

Set by Words & Graphics Ltd.
Anstey, Leicestershire
Printed and bound in Great Britain by
T. J. International Ltd., Padstow, Cornwall

This book is printed on acid-free paper

This book is for my beloved mother and
father, my brother David, my sisters Moira
and Tessa, my aunts Thea and Joan, and
my cousins Jinny, Prue and Simon. We
had so many happy days — I was lucky
to have such a family.

It is also for AW. We have been married now
for more than forty years, which is why, in
the pages that follow, I do not linger long
on my love life before the happy day
I met him.

And it is for my cherished daughters,
Hester and Claudia, in the hopes that their
childhood memories are as happy as mine.

# Introduction

A decade ago, I wrote a book about being married to a diplomat (*Diplomatic Baggage*, it was called) and someone gave a copy to my uncle. When he'd read it he said, 'Well, it's quite amusing, but it's all about *her*, isn't it.'

I have been worrying about those words since I started writing this new book because, though I don't think *Diplomatic Baggage* really *was* all about me, this one certainly is — but on the other hand, how on earth do you write a memoir and make it NOT about yourself? Readers will just have to believe me when I say that *Full Marks for Trying* is not meant to be a giant ego trip, but a picture of what it was like to grow up at a certain time in history — in the 1940s, '50s and '60s — in a family that was, like Britain itself, facing and adapting to the enormous changes taking place around us with gathering speed.

My parents' generation lived through the horrors and dramas of two world wars but only saw the beginnings of all the profound social, sexual, gender, medical, religious and technological changes that have altered the world since *my* generation came into being — which have been, perhaps, the greatest ever to take place in the course of any person's lifetime (so far).

I hadn't really thought much about this before I began *Full Marks for Trying*, but writing about

1

one's childhood and youth highlights the changes, because you can remember what it was like before they happened.

There are the obvious, mundane physical ones, of course — motorways, seat belts, air travel, London's changing skyline — and then there are more subtle ones: when I first came to live in London, Downing Street, now sealed off behind huge gates, was just another road — you could amble past Number 10 and stare at the policeman standing outside the door; similarly you could park, free, next to the stones at Stonehenge and go and touch them; the stunning Art Deco foyer of the Strand Palace Hotel *was* its foyer (now it belongs to the V&A Museum); and Wolseley was the name of a car and not a fashionable London restaurant in Piccadilly (where there used to be an old Wolseley garage, but everyone has forgotten that).

Then there are the humdrum domestic changes: duvets have replaced eiderdowns; tampons have taken over from sanitary towels and their ugly accompanying belts; hand-held hair dryers and heated rollers mean we no longer have to sleep in curlers. Disposable nappies have made redundant the whole rigmarole of towelling and muslin squares which had to be boiled on the stove because people didn't have washing machines. Kleenex tissues are the new handkerchiefs (the idea of blowing your nose into a piece of cloth was never nice, but on the other hand, hankies were such a useful Christmas gift, especially for men — though little girls like me were always being given flat boxes of pretty, embroidered ones which we hardly ever opened, let alone used).

We all know about tights replacing stockings and suspender belts, but there was a slightly earlier, almost forgotten, liberation when *seamless* stockings appeared for the first time. Stockings with seams sound sexy now, but they were a nuisance to put on — you had to guide the seam with your finger and thumb up the centre of the back of your leg and then, all day, you'd be looking over your shoulder to check, or asking friends: 'Are my seams straight?'

There were no credit cards in my youth, which meant cashing cheques all the time — usually at the bank, but at your local corner shop if you could persuade them — and persuading them was quite important because being stranded without money was a problem then as there was no easy way to get any.

In my day you couldn't go to the lavatory on a train when it was in a station because the flush drained out directly on to the tracks — which made us wonder what was happening with aeroplanes: was it all likely to come plopping down on our heads?

In 1977 Dad and my sister Tessa and I clubbed together to give Mum her first ever washing machine for her seventieth birthday — but instead of being pleased she was furious because she thought it was some kind of negative comment on the way she'd always done the washing before.

My in-laws had the first washing-up machine I

ever saw, but I was sceptical about it because they seemed to have to rinse all the plates before they put them in which I thought was kind of doing the same job twice.

The food we eat now would be unrecognisable back in the Fifties — I mean literally; few people then knew what an avocado pear looked like, let alone an artichoke, or a mango or passion fruit, or croissants, baguettes, wraps, pizza, sushi, or anything in a Tetra Pak. The nearest we got to hamburgers were found at a chain called Wimpy Bars and they were thin, stamped-out circles of grey something (mince would be too kind a word) in a tasteless white bun with a dollop of ketchup. Ice cream was served, not in a cone but in a slice between two wafers; spaghetti came in tins with tomato sauce — we knew so little about pasta in those days that in 1957 when Richard Dimbleby (the even-more-famous broadcasting father of David and Jonathan) made an April Fool film for *Panorama* about Italians gathering the 'spaghetti harvest', showing long strands draped over the branches of trees with cheery Italians on ladders 'picking' it, half the nation was taken in. Olive oil was only available in chemist's, where it was sold in small bottles for earache; and there was no yoghurt in the supermarkets — indeed there were no supermarkets.

When I started work in an office my typewriter was one of those big upright ones you see in old films on which the carriage made a rather satisfactory zip-and-clunk noise when you pushed it back. Then I graduated to an electric typewriter, and it was not until the early 2000s that I dared to write on a computer — and that was only because my daughters persuaded me to try.

Before Xerox machines were invented we usually did copying (text only) with carbon paper sandwiched between sheets of plain paper and fed into the typewriter, but also, more curiously, with an A4-sized shallow pan of hard jelly. You wrote with special ink on to a sheet of paper which was pressed on to the jelly: this absorbed the ink and would then reprint it on to any fresh piece of paper laid on top.

Computers were the size of sheds when I was in my twenties: universities and corporations hired them, and students and particular employees were allowed to use them for short periods — obviously no one had one at home, and no one had as yet even imagined a desk- or lap-top, let alone an iPad or tablet. As teenagers we fantasised about telephones which would show you the person at the other end of the line (I was not keen on the idea: I worried that someone might ring when I didn't have my make-up on) but we never believed that these might one day become the norm. We didn't even dream of the wonder of a telephone you could carry around with you, let alone a telephone you could carry that was a computer as well, i.e., a smartphone, let alone a smartphone in a *watch* . . . and there will probably — no, make that *definitely* — be something even more extraordinary coming up any minute now. In fact, I am not going to say any more about the vast, ongoing, world-changing revolutions in information technology because, for a start, I have no idea what most of them are as I can only just about manage emails and Facebook and Google.

There were curious medical conditions in the 1940s and '50s that don't seem to exist any more — 'glands' was one. I don't actually know what 'glands' were, but when someone was really fat, people would whisper: 'S/he's got *glands*.' When we came back from India, my sister Moira had to have an operation for fallen arches which meant both her legs being in plaster for weeks, though I've never heard of a single person having this done since. And then there were chilblains — does anyone get these now, I wonder?

When you went to the dentist in the Fifties there were no injections to numb the pain; instead they put a gas mask or a pad of ether over your face, and as you breathed in the fumes, you drifted into a sleep full of surreal and menacing happenings. My cousin Simon had an ether dream I've never forgotten — a terrifying clown was perched on the end of a long rope, swinging to and fro, chanting, and as it advanced and receded its voice got louder and then fainter: *ABRIco spiNICO ABrico SPINIco AbriCO SPinico ABRIco* . . .

But then there were the truly miraculous medical breakthroughs that have really transformed our lives. I came into the world at about the same time as antibiotics, but I was born long before chemotherapy changed the fate of cancer

6

sufferers, and before the discovery of the Salk vaccine, when polio was a real, terrifying threat and almost everyone knew a child who had been disabled by it, and had heard of the Iron Lung (a breathing apparatus for polio victims).

The birth-control pill became available in my lifetime, which meant that the dread of becoming an 'unmarried mother' which had haunted women forever because of all the terrible things that went with having an 'illegitimate baby' — disgrace, being cast out by your family, poverty, a backstreet abortion (during which you could die), having to give your baby away, homes for 'fallen women' — was becoming a thing of the past.

Our language was different: 'super' was the word for anything good or pleasant; I suppose it is 'cool' now (or 'sick' if you are really what we would have called 'with it'). Personnel was our word for Human Resources and I don't remember ever coming across someone called a line manager at work. People were crippled not disabled, half-caste instead of mixed race, Negro as opposed to black or of colour. 'Coming out' meant a girl coming-of-age and entering society, not declaring your sexuality to the world. Cohabiting unmarried couples were 'living in sin'; divorce was rare, and the word 'divorcee' for a divorced woman had a kind of racy ring to it . . . Being 'tight' was not being mean, but drunk — 'tight as a tick' meant really drunk. A pansy was a gay man; gay meant cheery, bright, fun. Poking someone meant having sex with them — I nearly had a fit when I first joined Facebook and people 'poked' me.

My favourite out-of-date expression, though, is 'playing the giddy ox' which Dad was always using — it meant mucking about, as in 'You girls, for heaven's sake stop playing the giddy ox and settle down to your homework.'

In the early Sixties girls were called 'birds' — which could be confusing: a young male friend of ours, staying in a village in France, invited his English neighbour, whom he didn't know, to supper. 'Can I bring my bird?' the man asked. 'Of course,' said our friend, thinking how nice it would be if a girl came along too, but he turned up with his pet chicken.

Even journalism changed: in 1963 Katharine Whitehorn published a column on 'sluts' in the *Observer* which altered the way women — or men for that matter — wrote. Katharine's definition of a slut was someone who took clothes out of the dirty laundry basket to wear because they were cleaner than the ones they had on, brushed their hair with someone else's nailbrush or changed their laddered stockings in a taxi. Until that column, journalists rarely wrote much in the first person, let alone about things like dirty underwear — in fact, the editor of the *Observer* made Katharine postpone publication of the slut piece until she had ceased being fashion editor of the paper. After 'sluts', journalism became much more personal and intimate, leading to the many newspaper columns about the writers' own lives that we have today — or, indeed, you could say, leading to this book.

There were no women newsreaders until the mid-Fifties (as a teenager I thought women could *never* do the job because their voices were not deep enough); there were no women pilots on commercial airlines until the 1960s; and in 1944 a film, *National Velvet*, was made about a girl (Elizabeth Taylor) dressing up as a young man in order to ride in the Grand National. In reality it was not until 1977 that the first woman jockey competed in that race.

In the Fifties, women wore skirts: jeans were still workwear for factory hands, miners and cowboys (James Dean wore them in *Rebel Without a Cause* to show just how rebellious he was). Trousers were called slacks, and were only worn by women for sport or on holiday. In fact, women wearing them were not *allowed* into more formal offices and restaurants; it wasn't until 1967, for instance, that a woman in trousers was permitted to eat in the restaurant of the Savoy Hotel. The difference a couple of decades has made in fashion is neatly illustrated by the wardrobes of female world leaders: Margaret Thatcher never wore trousers but Angela Merkel never wears anything else; Hillary Clinton was the first woman politician to wear trousers for her official portrait.

Last summer I found myself walking behind a group of girls in Oxford Street all wearing the shortest of shorts with bare legs, and I was suddenly struck by how they would be the stuff of heart attacks to anyone from the Fifties — even the Sixties — let alone further back in time. But this applies to so many things that we take for granted today . . . As for myself, I am just like the person who worked in a chocolate factory and never wants to eat chocolate again: having been so enthusiastic and so closely involved in fashion all through the Sixties and part of the Seventies, I find I can't take it that seriously any more.

Being Catholic, my family didn't eat meat on Fridays and fasted on Ash Wednesday and Good Friday — fasting meant you could only drink liquids; I used to wonder if it would count if I chopped up a whole meal and put it into my aunt's new mixer and then drank it like a milkshake. When we went to Mass we had to cover our hair with a headscarf, and if we were going to communion we had to fast for an hour beforehand, which meant that if you were late getting up for Mass you couldn't have breakfast. You were never allowed to touch the communion wafer, or host as it is called: at communion, it was put on our tongues. A nun at school told me that if a host dropped on the floor you would have to lick it up. And you definitely couldn't go to communion if you had committed a Mortal Sin (this was the core of the plot of Graham Greene's 1948 novel *The Heart of the Matter*).

Now all that is out of the window: no head covering, no fasting, the host is placed in your hand, and I don't think most ordinary Catholics — as opposed to Mafia mob members, perhaps? — worry very much about mortal sins these days.

Perhaps that's because even SINS seem to

have changed: all the things that we were taught were wicked (and some of them were *illegal* in those days as well) — sex outside marriage, contraception, homosexuality, abortion, masturbation — are now discussed openly and chattily in the *Guardian*'s 'Sexual Healing' column.

So there we are — a glimpse at what was going on in the background of *Full Marks for Trying*. It was a very different, much less complicated world (with less than half the people on earth than there are today) which I hope that older people might recognise and younger ones will find interesting. But, as well, I hope that readers will find themselves in some of my memories — for I was not the only child who came 'home' to a grim post-war England after a Technicolor childhood in one of England's colonies, nor the only one to be a self-conscious and unattractive teenager, nor the only one blundering along in life, making mistakes; not the only girl who straightened her stocking seams in the Fifties, revelled in the bold new fashions of the Sixties or, to her parents' despair, didn't get married until over thirty.

Of course not everything that happened to me as I grew up is here — for a start there is lots I don't remember, some that I don't particularly want to remember, and masses that is tedious and dull and deserved to be left out. And not all the important events that happened in fashion in the Sixties are recorded here either, just the ones that affected me personally.

Note: In India nearly all the place names that I knew as a child have been changed. I have used the old names, but with the modern name as well when it is not obvious.

# 1

To tell the truth, I have never felt completely at home in my homeland, England. Deep down there's always been a tinge of anxiety, almost guilt: a feeling that I don't really fit in and am not quite adequate or up to the mark in some subtle way; it's how you feel at school when you know you are not in the cool group — or as a grown-up when you read *Tatler* magazine. My daughter Hester feels the same and puts it rather well: 'It's as if the English all know a secret that we don't — and they know we don't, but are not going to tell it to us.'

The source of our insecurity is easily found — in the Jesuit sayings about the importance of early childhood: 'Give me a child until the age of seven,' goes one version, 'and I will make him mine for ever.' And there we have it — the reason I don't feel at home in England is obviously because I belong to India where I lived until I was eight years old. (Hester was raised in Brussels.)

I was born in the British Military Hospital in a place called Ambala, about 125 miles north of Delhi. Ambala sits pretty much at the centre of the ancient Grand Trunk Road which crosses the widest, top part of the triangle of India, going 2,500 miles from the Bay of Bengal, through Bangladesh, India, and then Pakistan, to Afghanistan (or the other way round), and so it was a

13

natural place for the British, in the nineteenth century, to set up an army base, or cantonment as they are known in India (pronounced cantoonment). My father, who was in the Indian Army (Dogra Regiment), was posted there with Mum at the time I arrived in the world — which was in November 1939. Since India became independent only eight years later, and there was a world war which separated couples in between, I must be among the last of the British Raj babies, along with a few others of my age, the best-known of whom are Joanna Lumley, who was born in Srinagar, Kashmir, because her dad (like mine) was in the army (a Gurkha of course), and Julie Christie, born in Assam, because her father was a tea planter. (In older generations, Spike Milligan and Vivien Leigh were born in India, and I was once assured that Elizabeth Taylor had been born in Calcutta, but when I looked it up it turned out her birthplace was nowhere more exotic than Hampstead Garden Suburb.)

The India that I feel I belong to no longer exists because it was the India of the last days of the British Raj and can only be glimpsed in photographs and films now, but then again, no place is the same as it was seventy-five years ago, and the all-white England we 'Indian' children felt so ill-at-ease in when we were brought home does not exist either, thank heavens. Curiously, though, no matter the changes, I have to say that for me those old Jesuits were right: I still feel nostalgic for the time and the country in which I spent my early years, and I still feel very much at home in India.

I should have grown up to be a spy because I learned recently that 'Kim' Philby, the notorious British double agent, was also born in Ambala, in 1912. He was actually called Harold Adrian Russell but nicknamed 'Kim' after the boy in Rudyard Kipling's book of the same name, and the irony is that the Kim in the novel was also involved with the British Secret Services, being tasked with delivering a message to the Head of Intelligence — in Ambala of all places, of course. And weirdest of all, when reading his obituary not long ago, I discovered that Harry Chapman Pincher, the well-known British journalist who made a whole long career out of writing about spies, was also born in Ambala.

But I didn't turn into a spy; I did something very slightly similar by becoming a journalist, and then marrying a diplomat — I call my husband AW — and in 1986 we were posted to India where I immediately felt as if I belonged (despite living in a hotel room for months) but where AW and our daughters took a while to settle down.

Later, long after we had left India and were posted to Syria, AW and I went back on a visit, partly because our daughter Hester was doing a gap year there, and partly so that AW, who is a Buddhist, could visit Dharamsala where the Dalai Lama has his base. We hired a battered old taxi in Delhi for the journey to Dharamsala and at one point our route actually took us through Ambala — where the driver fell asleep and we very nearly had a head-on collision with a lorry which would have been fatal. AW said my obituary would have read 'Brigid Keenan, born in Ambala 1939, died in Ambala 1994', and people would think I had never left the place in between.

⋆   ⋆   ⋆

My brother and sisters and I grew up aware that our family had been in India for a long time — at least four generations we were told — as railway engineers (my grandfather), army and customs (other grandfather), railway administration (great-grandfather), foresters (uncle), indigo planters (great-great-uncle). Furthest back, and most romantically, was a Frenchman, E. Dubus, apparently taken prisoner by the British in Bengal during the Napoleonic Wars, who was allowed to return to France for a year, on parole, in order to bring his silk-weaving business back to India from Lyons. He set up his factory, which was called Nakanda, in Bengal. I inherited a drawing he made of the building and in 2014 AW and I went — armed with a copy of the picture — to the once-French settlement of Chandernagore near Calcutta, and to various silk-weaving areas in the region trying, and failing, to find Nakanda. We came to the conclusion that perhaps it was in the part of Bengal which is now Bangladesh. We are still on the case. (What we *have* found, among Mum's and Dad's old family papers, is the marriage certificate of E. Dubus's daughter Madeleine (my great-grandmother) to an Englishman, Walter Charles Lydiard — another silk manufacturer in Bengal — in 1872 in India.)

Dad himself was born in Bangalore in 1902; we were always urging him to write down his memoirs for us but he only managed about half a dozen pages scrawled on the backs of envelopes or on already-used scrap paper, briefly telling how, soon after he was born, his family moved to Burma where his father worked for Customs and Excise; how they moved back to Bangalore in 1912 so their five children could go to school (nowhere suitable in Rangoon); how his father volunteered for the army in the First World War and was posted to Basra in Iraq (Dad's mother stayed in Bangalore with the children); and how Dad went to England when he was seventeen, swotted like mad at an army crammer and got into Sandhurst, after which he returned to serve in the Indian Army. (His parents eventually resumed their old life in Burma.)

My father lists these bare facts, but he writes a little more about two other, obviously rather traumatic and therefore memorable, events in his life. One was being bitten by a rabid dog when he was a young soldier of twenty-three, and having to go to the Pasteur Institute in Kasauli, 'in the hills' (as people referred to the Himalayas), and endure two injections with a huge needle into his stomach, one on each side of his navel, every day for fourteen days. The other was how his grandfather, an elderly widower who had retired from the Great Indian

Peninsula Railway to the Nilgiri Hills in south-western India, married the nurse who cared for him in hospital there when he developed pneumonia. She was called Mrs White. Dad went to stay with the newlyweds when he was in the Nilgiri Hills himself, convalescing from the rabies injections, but after that the family don't seem to have heard much from them again, and when the old man died a couple of years later, he left everything to his new wife. This must have been a bitter blow to the family: Dad wrote that his grandfather had a 'fat' pension, and he'd been impressed by what he saw on his visit to them. 'He [the grandfather] had acquired some acres of Shola forest which he cleared and turned into a very pleasant estate with a fully furnished and well-built house, servants' quarters, outbuildings, full staff and a motor car with driver.' Not a single penny — or perhaps I should say rupee — of all this was passed to Dad's family. Mrs White was never forgotten by the Keenans . . . An odd postscript to the story is that this grandfather and my mother's grandfather are buried practically side by side in the Christian cemetery of Ootacamund in the Nilgiri Hills: they did not know each other in their lifetimes, but two generations later their descendants married, and they themselves ended up neighbours in death.

★  ★  ★

Since Dad never got round to the memoirs, I can only follow our progress round India via the family photograph albums, and I see from the pictures taken at my christening in Ambala that, aside from the fact that I was a truly *hideous* baby, we lived in a rather pleasant, colonial-style white bungalow with a deep veranda enclosed by arches. There seems to be someone called Nanny in these pictures, but she never appears again, and I never heard her talked about. My half-brother David — eleven years older than me (his father was Mum's first husband who died not long after David was born) — was at school in England so she was not there for him; perhaps she looked after my sister Moira, who was seven when I was born, or maybe she was just taken on as a maternity nurse for my own first few weeks.

We obviously didn't stay long in Ambala because six months later, on the next page of the album, in 1940, we are in Kasauli, where Dad had had his anti-rabies injections fifteen years before. I learn from Google that Kasauli is not only another army cantonment town, it is also a popular Indian holiday resort, so maybe we were just there on leave, because, on the following page, again only a few months later, we have moved to Jubbulpore (now called Jabalpur), an ancient town in central India with a large army cantonment and a strange history: it was chosen as the base of operations for Sir William Henry Sleeman, a British soldier and administrator, who, in the 1830s, suppressed the Thuggee cult in India. Thuggees (it's where our word 'thug' comes from) had terrorised the country for six hundred years: they would befriend travellers and then, having gained their confidence, they would strangle them, steal their possessions and bury their bodies by the road. Thousands were killed in this way, and it was all done in the spirit of making a sacrifice to the god Kali. Jabalpur is also one of the places where, notoriously, Indian mutineers/freedom fighters were executed by cannon in 1857.

There are five pages in the album of me with Mum and Moira in Jabalpur in 1941 doing various things in our garden — sitting on a horse held by a *syce*, the Indian word for a groom (see the cover of this book), petting a small spotted deer that I have no recollection of at all and posing beside a beautiful vintage car (which was of course just a normal car in those days). Next thing, I am at a tea party far away from there in Kashmir, dressed as the White Rabbit from *Alice in Wonderland*. (The other day I visited my oldest friend, Sophie, who was born in India the year after me; we were going through her photo album and suddenly there was a picture of Sophie, aged two, at a party, also dressed as the White Rabbit — her costume looks uncannily like mine so we came to the conclusion that my mother must have passed it on to her mother.)

After Kashmir we are in the hill station of Nathia Gali (in what is now Pakistan) and for the first time since my christening — because it was wartime and he was always away — Dad is in the pictures with Moira and me, so he must have come home on leave. Then we seem to have passed briefly through a place called Kalabagh before moving to Peshawar (also now in Pakistan) because Dad was posted to the

North-West Frontier, and that is where my younger sister Tessa was born in 1942. (Dad knew about all the secret military tunnels and fortifications in the hills around the Frontier, and when we were older we used to tease him by calling him Keenan of the Khyber.)

And then, suddenly, it is 1945, and we are photographed in the garden of our grandparents' house in England. I will explain that later.

I don't know why we moved seven times in four years but it's no wonder I have so many dim memories of travelling on Indian trains: of journeys that took days not hours, of being shepherded through the clamour and confusion at the stations, of the vendors crowding round with food or ingenious toys made of clay or wood and string (they still do, but the toys are all plastic these days), of the meals — ordered in advance at previous stations — that came with white cloths and napkins and were brought to our carriage by uniformed bearers (waiters). There was no air-conditioning then so big blocks of ice were heaved into the carriages and placed on the floor and we children would sit on them while they slowly melted. On one of these journeys Mum pulled the communication cord on the train — I was grown up enough by then to be terrified that she would be arrested and taken away. It happened when we were settling back in our carriage after a halt: Mum accidentally kicked her shoe out of the door and on to the track. There was no question of retrieving it because, by the time she realised what had happened, we had gathered speed and were out of the station and well on our way, so she grabbed the cord — and amazingly, the train grumbled to a stop with much screeching and grinding of brakes and wheels. There were signs all over the carriages warning of the penalties you faced if you pulled the cord unnecessarily, but though railway officials — the guard? the driver? — came and there were questions and explanations, someone found her shoe and our journey was resumed and, phew, Mum was not dragged away in chains.

I feared for her another time, later on, when the police came to our house because there had been a fight between our cook and the vegetable *wallah*. It turned out to have been all Mum's fault — she was writing letters home when the cook came to tell her that the vegetable *wallah* was at the door and Mum said, 'Oh I could kill the vegetable man, he always comes at the wrong time.'

It was a Thomas à Becket situation — the cook went out to kill the veg man on Mum's behalf and a big fight ensued, and when the police came and arrested the cook he said he was only acting on his memsahib's instructions. The police interviewed the various people involved (not, obviously, in front of us children) and, once again, I was terrified Mum would be hauled off to prison, but to everyone's relief, it was all sorted out and neither Mum nor the cook nor the vegetable *wallah* were arrested.

★   ★   ★

Apart from the break in 1945 when we went back to England for a time, my family stayed in India until 1948, a year after Independence, when we, like all the other British who'd lived there, had to pack up and go 'home'. Hollow laughter here as 'home' was the place we children knew least in the world, though people in India talked about it a lot in a yearning way: there were cherished 'letters from home', longed-for 'news from home', and there were those who, excitingly, had come from 'home' or were going 'home'. We thought 'home' must be something like heaven.

Until recently, I had no idea when in 1948 we left India, but then I discovered a site on the internet (www.passengerlists.co.uk) which specialises in obscure ships' passenger lists, and it tracked down the Keenan family on SS *Franconia*, sailing from Bombay for Liverpool in June that year. From a photocopy of the document I found that my mother, who seemed old to us, was only forty when we came home, and that almost everyone on board our ship — more than a thousand people — belonged to British families exactly like ours; not necessarily army folk, of course, but missionaries, office workers, tea planters, a dressmaker, telephonists, typists, engineers and nurses as well. They had nearly all written 'India' or 'Pakistan' in the column headed Country of Last *Permanent* Residence (my italics) and that made me feel sad because it represented so much upheaval, parting and heartbreak . . . I also discovered lately (from the British Association for Cemeteries in South Asia) that there are perhaps two *million*

British graves in India — of those whose names would never be on any returning ships' passenger lists.

One of our own addresses in India seems to be etched on my brain, probably because I was at that age — seven? — when I wrote it obsessively in all my books: Brightlands, 219A Bolton Road, Secunderabad, Deccan, India, The World, The Universe. Not long ago, on another return visit to India, AW and I were on a train going to Delhi and met a charming young Indian woman with a BlackBerry and she somehow looked it up — the street names are Indianised these days, of course, but she managed to find it — and discovered that our bungalow, Brightlands, is now a venue for wedding receptions.

*   *   *

What took a good few of our ancestors to India (along with very many other young men in a similar situation) was being poor in Ireland and joining the British Army which, apart from the Guinness Brewery, was one of the main employers there. (Roddy Doyle once described this as the great unspoken secret in Ireland.) And so, ironically, colonised Irishmen became part of the colonisation of India. Kipling chose to give two of his most famous characters this background: Terence Mulvaney, an irreverent troublemaking soldier who comes into many short stories, and, of course, Kim himself, whose real name in the book was Kimball O'Hara — the orphan child of an impoverished Irish

24

soldier serving in India, and his wife.

★ ★ ★

I thought I'd been told that my Keenan great-grandfather married his wife in the cathedral in Bangalore, so a few years ago, when I first decided to investigate my family in India, I wrote to the Archbishop of Bangalore to ask if anyone there could look for the marriage certificate. He kindly went through the records and found not my great-grandfather's, but four *other* marriages at the end of the nineteenth century involving Keenan girls from our family — with a British Army corporal, two sergeants and a drum-major. One of them, Bridget, was my great-aunt (why she spelled her name in the English and not the Irish way I don't know).

By the time I was born our family had risen in rank, and our life in India, and indeed the lives of all the British officers who served in the Indian Army in the last days of the Raj, was perfectly described by Paul Scott in his novel *The Jewel in the Crown*. We didn't actually have a Hari Kumar-type illicit love affair and trauma in our midst, but I often think that had my sisters and I been born fifteen or twenty years earlier, any of us might have been Daphne Manners or Sarah Layton and created scandal and drama by falling in love with an Indian, a 'native'.

We children always took the Indian side in any argument or disagreement with the staff in the house, and I used to be upset that the store cupboard in the kitchen containing tea and coffee, sugar and flour, was kept locked and that Mum doled out what was needed, and that Dad sometimes marked the whisky bottle so he'd know if someone had swigged a secret tot — though I found it incredibly clever that he used to turn the bottle upside down and *then* mark it so that the secret sign would not be where a person would expect it.

Our grandfather, we were told, had a foolproof method for detecting which of his servants had stolen something. If anything important went missing, he would summon all the staff and give them each a straw or a taper of the same length, and tell them that overnight the straw belonging to the thief would grow an inch. The next day he would summon them again — and find one straw *shortened* by an inch — which belonged, of course, to the culprit. I used to wonder about this, because you could probably only do it once.

In my mind's eye my handsome father (black hair, blue eyes, very Irish-looking — with an Irish temper to match) is always dressed in stiffly ironed knee-length khaki shorts, with a shiny leather Sam Browne belt and long socks. He had a moustache (I've always loved men with moustaches as a consequence, I suppose) and when we were growing up Dad used to say, 'Kissing a man without a moustache is like eating a hard-boiled egg without salt' — but AW had a moustache when I married him, and when he shaved it off I didn't notice for more than a month.

The mental picture I have of my mother then

is very 1940s (not surprising because it *was* the 1940s): she has streaky light-brown hair rolled up away from her face like a Hollywood film star of the time, and she is sitting at a dressing table (people don't seem to have dressing tables any more, the same way they don't use tea sets) wearing a robe in some floppy material, and leaning forward — either to wipe Pond's Cold Cream off her face with a wodge of cotton wool, or to stroke bright red lipstick on to her big smiley mouth stretched open for this purpose in an O. Mum had pretty hands with tapering fingers — I got Dad's wrinkled stubby ones in the DNA lottery, as well as a husky croak instead of her lovely singing voice. She played the piano, and used to entertain us with Kipling's poems set to music, or mournful Irish ballads. Her favourite was about an emigrant who is leaving Ireland for the United States but his girlfriend hasn't turned up to say goodbye. 'Oh Kathleen Mavourneen, my sad tears are falling/To think that from Erin and thee I must part.' Then there was another about a child who has a nightmare that her father will be killed in a mining accident: 'So tell your mates of my dreams, Daddy/For sure as the stars that shine/Something is going to happen today/So Daddy, don't go down the mine.' And yet another about a dying child: 'Will I be an angel, Mother? An angel in the sky?' Sometimes Dad used to sing to Mum, always one of two songs — 'If You Were the Only Girl in the World' and 'Lady Be Good' — and though he'd fling his arms out in a jokey dramatic way, we knew that he meant every single word.

Like Dad, Mum was born and mostly raised in India until she was a teenager when she was sent to a convent in Ipswich where, she told us, the girls had to wear thin cotton shifts in the bath in case they themselves, or — worse — any other girl, saw their bodies. It was at this convent that my mother overheard the most popular girl in the school complaining to her pals that too many people wanted to be in their group. 'We've got to draw the line somewhere,' the girl said, 'so we'll draw it at Maisie Moss' (my mum).

When she was a child in Madras (now Chennai) Mum's father kept a pet monkey — a big gibbon called Jacko which had the run of the house. Mum was scared stiff of him, but she loved telling us how he once snatched my grandmother's cut-glass butter dish off the breakfast table and then climbed the tallest tree in the garden with it, licking the butter. Granny made everyone stand round the tree holding out sheets so that when Jacko finished his feast, got bored and dropped the dish, it would fall into the stretched-out cotton and wouldn't break; Jacko seemed to understand what was up, Mum said, and took hours revelling in the attention before he let the dish go. I don't remember what exactly happened in the end, but it must have fallen safely into the sheets because it was always on *our* breakfast table in India, inspiring Mum to tell the story.

Mum's first husband died (of septicaemia) when she was just twenty-one after only a year of marriage, and her younger brother Dick had joined the International Brigades and gone to fight in the Civil War in Spain where he had disappeared (the family lived in desperate hope that news of him would come one day), but she was unbowed: glamorous and clever and fun and full of laughter, and in those days she was up for anything. Before she became pregnant with me, for instance, she went all the way back to England from India by bus with six-year-old Moira, my sister, so that she could buy a quilted coat in Damascus en route (it was in the dressing-up box for years). In the modern world she would have had a good job — I always imagine she might have been at the BBC or on a newspaper, but she could have been a teacher too; as it was, she wrote a couple of children's books for Tessa and me, and ran a small nursery school at home in England (until we moved, when she had to close it again); she painted well, designed and stitched beautiful needlepoint tapestries, was an excellent dressmaker, worked as a guide for NADFAS (National Association of Decorative and Fine Arts Societies), played bridge and was very good at making all our temporary houses look nice, with no money. I adored her and Dad, and will always miss them and be grateful to them for passing on their energy and enthusiasm for life. Mum used Chanel No. 5 — it was her annual birthday/ Christmas present from Dad — and I still have the spray bottle that was on her dressing table when she died. I don't allow myself to smell it because it makes her loss too painful, even now, more than twenty years on.

★　★　★

Our childhood was very ordered: we lived in the type of bungalows you can still see in the old cantonment areas (now of course used by the Indian military); everyone around us wore a khaki uniform; and our surroundings were immaculately tidy and well-organised. The trees were whitewashed from their waists down and the bricks edging the paths were painted white, and the hard brown earth was perpetually being swept with grass brooms (the sound of gentle sweeping is the background noise of my childhood, along with cawing crows). There was nearly always a Lutyens-style redbrick church somewhere in each compound, so any time I find myself driving through Larkhill, the military town on Salisbury Plain, I am reminded of the cantonments in India because there is one there too.

Our houses had deep verandas for shade, and inside, the chick blinds at the windows were kept rolled down and sprinkled with water for coolness, so that we lived in semi-darkness with the dazzling glare outside filtered through finely split bamboo. The houses were quiet, with the ceiling fans whirring round in a whisper, and the staff and us children padding about in bare feet — but round at the back, by the kitchen area with its fire and beaten-earth floor, where we spent a good deal of time with our ayah, there was always a hubbub of servants and chat.

Most of the indoor quietness was because Tessa and I had no friends — I suppose this was because we didn't go to school; we were too young to be sent off somewhere outside the cantonment: Mum taught us reading and writing at home. To this day, more or less the only history I can remember is (in rhyme) from a children's book called *Kings and Queens*: 'So the Barons brought a Deed/Down to rushy Runnymede/Magna Carta was it hight/Charter of the People's right . . . 'Sign! Sign! Sign!' they said./'Sign, King John, or resign instead.''

Of course, among their army colleagues, our parents had lots of friends with children, and once in a while we would meet up with them for marvellous picnics or excursions, but these depended on our families finding themselves in the same postings. Tessa and I had each other and didn't miss friends — though later when we were in Poona (now Pune) and actually had one (Angeli Dev, the local doctor's daughter), we realised it could be fun. (Mum also made a friend in Poona, a Parsee lady called Siloo Cama; they stayed in touch for years and years: Mrs Cama used to come and stay in England wearing saris, bringing a touch of our beloved India as well as exotic presents like glass bangles for us girls; we liked her a lot.)

At one point I made up an imaginary friend called Ann Brown, but this was not out of loneliness, it was to make myself seem deeper and more interesting to the grown-ups. When I announced her existence — 'I've got a friend, she's called Ann Brown, but *you* can't see her or hear her, only I can' — their attention lasted long enough to say, 'How nice for you, darling,' so I gradually phased Ann Brown out and never referred to her again.

★ ★ ★

Because it was an army base, a cantonment housed everyone and everything the military might need — mechanics, cooks, cleaners, grooms, gardeners, soldiers, weapons I suppose, vehicles of all sorts — but best of all were the animal lines where the horses, mules and donkeys were kept. One of the songs Mum used to sing us was a Kipling poem called (I found out when I grew up) 'Parade-Song of the Camp-Animals', and it somehow brought the distant war closer to us children because we'd often be taken to see the animals Kipling was writing about, in our own base. 'See our line across the plain,/Like a heel-rope bent again,/ Reaching, writhing, rolling far,/Sweeping all away to war!/While the men that walk beside,/ Dusty, silent, heavy-eyed,/Cannot tell why we or they/March and suffer day by day.'

Kipling would have been very pleased to see the memorial to the animals killed in war in Hyde Park.

★ ★ ★

Our fruit and veg were always washed in a solution of permanganate of potash which coloured the water pink — *pinky pani* they called it — and our milk, in a jug with a net cover weighted down with beads, was always boiled so it had thick skin on it (which I loved). In some of the houses we lived in, the furniture stood in saucers of paraffin or water to stop ants getting to the wooden legs and eating them, and all of us slept under cotton mosquito nets, which was the cosiest thing — you were in your own safe space where no spiders or snakes or bugs could get at you. I would have liked to wrap myself in a mosquito net all day long. We must, at some stage, have lived in a house or houses without electricity because in the evenings Tessa and I sat at a table with a paraffin lamp on it — having our supper? doing lessons? — and to our horror swarms of fleshy flying ants flew blindly into it and us, and I have a mental picture of a *punkah wallah*, or fan man, squatting on the veranda pulling a string with his toe to make the banner of cloth hung across the ceiling of the sitting room swing to and fro causing a breeze, but maybe I have just seen that in a picture somewhere. It is hard to know, seventy years on, what the true memories are, and what are family legends and stories, or things seen in books, that have implanted themselves as memories. I am determined to keep things accurate, but does it matter?

★   ★   ★

For some time — I don't know if it was weeks or months — we lived a life of total bliss (as far as I was concerned anyway) in a tented military encampment with both Mum and Dad. It was in a place in the hills called Wah in what is now

33

Pakistan, but I have no idea why we were there or what Dad was doing, and strangely there are no photos of us in tents in the album. All I know is that we had a dining-room tent, a sitting-room tent, bedroom tents and bathroom tents, all connected by tent corridors, rather like a spreading one-storey card house. Some of the tents leaked and there were buckets to catch the drops, but that just seemed like part of the excitement to me. My sister Moira, who must have been about eleven or twelve then (I was four or five), took me for walks in the pine woods around the camp and we found a little cave in a mossy bank which became my doll's house for the remaining time we were there. We spent entirely happy days together furnishing it with bits of twig and stones for chairs and tables and furry leaves for bedcovers. Maybe the cave was where my enthusiasm for doing up houses was born — this became a positive obsession a couple of years later when I read the Little Grey Rabbit books. Grey Rabbit's home was my dream: it was so pretty and cosy and secure and stable — all I wanted was to live in a house like hers. It occurred to me the other day that, in fact, I have tried to make every house I've lived in look like Grey Rabbit's, with white paint on the walls, pretty plates on a kitchen dresser, crisp bedspreads, patchwork and gingham. Forget Kevin McCloud or *World of Interiors*, my design guru has always been Little Grey Rabbit.

Our tented camp was near Taxila, the well-known archaeological site dating back to the sixth century BC (now a UNESCO monument).

We were taken there one day by Mum and Dad who explained its history as we went around the ruins, and then Moira found an old bead in the mud and people got genuinely excited and crowded round to look, and I was sick with jealousy until I came across the dirty, dried-up old core of a sweetcorn cob and everyone told me that it was an amazing find, and how astonishingly clever and sharp-eyed I was, but I knew they were only trying to make me feel better.

★   ★   ★

India gets cold in winter but it seems to me now that my sisters and I only ever wore light cotton frocks with matching knickers because of the intense heat, and when the monsoon rains came, we flung off the dresses and ran out into the garden and danced wildly in the downpour, and breathed in that wonderful smell of water on parched earth which haunts everyone who has ever lived in a hot country. Our gardens were dusty and bare, with rows and rows of plants in terracotta pots, but the lawn area and flowerbeds were surrounded by little mud walls so that when, every evening, the *mali* (gardener) flooded them with the hose, no water escaped, and they were green.

In our day the population of India was four times less than it is now — only 350 million instead of 1.28 billion — and there was enough space for houses, even in military compounds, to have quite large, rambling gardens — with snakes. As Rumer Godden's novel *The River* tells so heartbreakingly, snakes were a real and present danger to young children in India, and my parents would, once in a while, hire a snake charmer to come and gather them up, much as you would get the council to send someone to deal with a rat problem in England. Snakes were my horror, my nightmare, my worst terror; we came across them quite often in the garden, and sometimes they would venture into the house so we always had to tap out our shoes for snakes and scorpions before putting them on. When I heard about St Patrick driving all the snakes out of Ireland I yearned to live there more than anything.

Kipling's story of 'Rikki-Tikki-Tavi', in which Nag the cobra and his wife plot to kill the little English family — exactly like ours — in whose garden they live, scares me even now. Cobras were our greatest fear, though we were also taught to watch out for the small but deadly banded krait, aka the seven-step snake because if you are bitten by it you can only take seven steps before you drop dead. Tessa and I made up a song about it: 'The banded krait/Has every right/To bite you in/The middle of the night/If you go out without a light/The banded krait/Has every right . . . ' and so on . . . and on and on; we would chant it in the car on long journeys, driving our parents mad.

*   *   *

My elder sister Moira used to say that our life in India was in Technicolor, and that after we

36

returned to Britain it was all in grim black and white, and this is true, but there was an underlying dark side as well. In fact I was often afraid: our childhood took place in the tumultuous years around Indian Independence and Partition, and I was horribly aware, even as a seven or eight year old, of our family being part of a tiny privileged white minority in a vast hostile world which wanted to get rid of us, and in which anything might happen at any moment. I was pretty certain that I would end up a penniless orphan like the poor beggar children we saw every time we went out of our compound (after all, why them and not me?) and I used to practise wearing my nightie in different ways — with a belt round the waist or my mother's scarf round the neck — so that if it was the only garment left to me, I would still manage to look like a respectable person.

And then of course there were the terrifying things that had happened to us British during our history in India — and how did anyone know they might not happen again? I tried to work out how, by lying on the floor with my face near the window, I could have been one of the survivors of the notorious Black Hole of Calcutta where, the story goes, more than a hundred British prisoners held overnight nearly all suffocated and died, or I would imagine myself rushing about being helpful among the 1,280 men, women and children trapped in the Siege of Lucknow for nearly five months, so that they'd make sure I got some food. (Later, whenever we played charades — which we did for years — there would nearly always be a scene from the Siege of Lucknow with someone playing the part of the young Scottish girl who first hears the bagpipes of the Scottish Highlanders in General Havelock's relieving force. Our young Aunt Joan was fond of this role, crying, 'Dinna ye hear it? Dinna ye hear it? The pipes of Lucknow . . . ' — words which I only discovered lately were wrongly quoted from a poem by an American, John Greenleaf Whittier, which had made the relief of Lucknow famous for decades.)

Mysterious and scary things happened in India: we learned about the Indian Rope Trick in which (the story goes) a travelling magician hurls a rope high into the air — so far up you can't see the end of it — which stays there with no support, and then a child climbs up and disappears. And we heard about our mother's friend who was asked for a lock of her hair by a fortune teller who came to her house. Not wanting to hand over something so intimate, she cut a tiny wisp from a reddish fur rug she had, and gave that instead. That night she was woken by the swishing sound of the fur rug slowly sliding out of the bedroom — if she'd given her hair, of course, it would have been *her* . . .

One breakfast time our parents told us about the magnificent dinner they'd been to the night before, given by some rajah, at which the entertainment was men putting skewers through their cheeks and tongues and arms and legs — allegedly magically, with no blood or cuts or pain. But we heard Mum and Dad discussing it later and it seemed that as they drove away at the end of the evening they had noticed several men lying at the side of the driveway and worried that they were the supposedly uninjured performers who had done the tricks.

There was a time when we used to drive for picnics to a beauty spot where there was an ancient well — it was supposed to be haunted by the ghost of a daredevil British officer who had tried to jump over it on his horse but missed, so he and his mount plunged into the black depths of the water, many feet below. The well was in the middle of nowhere and shadowed by a tree hung with the weird, alien, nests of weaver-birds — like tubular flasks made of woven grass — and we once saw a big snake slide away into the undergrowth. I thought it was a sinister place, and I hated going there; sometimes it comes into my dreams even now.

★   ★   ★

When my new baby sister Tessa suddenly appeared out of nowhere in the winter of 1942, I was furiously jealous, and angry at how all the grown-ups spent so much time cooing over her and saying how exactly like my father she was. But then there was a terrible panic when she nearly died because *I had poisoned her*. I don't think I intended to kill Tessa, but it seems that, under interrogation, I told my mother that she had liked the berries I fed her, but not the paper, or perhaps it was the other way around. Tessa was tiny, and desperately sick, and had to be given a teaspoon of water every half hour through the days and nights, and Mum was in a complete panic because Ayah had gone on leave, home to Madras, and there was no one to help her — and then an odd thing happened: Ayah suddenly reappeared saying that on the train home she'd had a feeling her babies needed her so she'd turned around and come back.

Whether it was berries or paper that nearly killed Tessa, she recovered, thank heavens; I don't know how I would have managed the first part of my life without her and Moira and their jokes and companionship. In Amsterdam there is a bridge over a canal built by two sisters who lived on opposite sides of the water but couldn't bear to be separated — I understand that completely. Because of my siblings, when I was women's editor of the *Observer* back in the 1970s, I once devoted my page to investigating the sisterly relationship — and discovered that not everyone feels as I do. We talked to lots of sisters, including Brigitte Bardot's, Edith Piaf's (half-sister) and Glenda Jackson's (if we were doing the piece now we'd definitely be trying to question Pippa Middleton) — but best of all, we spoke to the famous Mitfords. First I asked Nancy, the eldest, about her relationship with the others, and she said, 'Sisters stand between you and life's misfortunes.' Then I talked to Jessica, the youngest Mitford, living in the US. 'What did Nancy say?' she asked. I told her, and she said, 'But Nancy WAS life's misfortunes to the rest of us.'

# 2

As I have mentioned before, Tessa's and my childhood in India was in two parts, with a break in the middle in 1945 when Mum returned to England with us, her three daughters (Moira never went back to India) — and that's when we were photographed in our grandparents' garden.

There was a desperately urgent reason for us to go home then: Mum and Dad had left David, her son, our half-brother, at prep school in England in 1938 when he was ten, expecting to see him two years later. In those days, because of the time it took to travel, military people overseas had a long leave every *second* year, meaning that, heartbreaking though it was, a two-year separation was more or less normal — but the world war broke out in 1939 and it was not possible for Mum to get back. By 1945, when the fighting in Europe eventually came to an end, Mum had not seen David for SEVEN years and could not wait one more moment: our passages home were booked, despite the fact that the war with Japan continued and that Dad was in Burma and now about to be posted on to the Middle East.

The saddest event of my childhood was losing my ayah at this time. For some reason (and who knows? maybe they were right) my parents thought that it would be better not to warn Ayah or me in advance that we were about to be

41

separated for ever, so we only found out what was to happen the very morning it did — when the car came to take the family off to the station to begin our journey 'home', first to Bombay and then to England, leaving Ayah behind to return to Madras, never to be seen again. Compared to the pain and grief of Mum's separation from David, the loss of my Ayah-Ma, as I called her, must have seemed fairly insignificant to everyone else, but to me it was a calamity.

Ayah and I screamed as we were, literally, pulled apart; I can still hear the sound and feel the pain. We had been together for nearly six years: when I was very small I used to lie in the hammock made in her lap by the cotton sari stretched between her knees as she sat cross-legged on the floor of the kitchen, while she fed me bits of chapatti dipped in honey. (Little did I know that life could only go downhill from then onwards.) Our parents were hands-on people, but Ayah-Ma had been my support and protector, my dark guardian angel; never bored or cross or critical, because in her eyes I was incapable of doing wrong. I remember her hands more than anything; small and strong, they were far more versatile than European ones: Ayah's hands could curl round to form a watertight drinking bowl, or they could splash drops of water over you in the bath as efficiently as a shower, or they could become a cloth to wipe away tears or pinch the snot off the end of your nose; her wiry brown fingers could be tweezers, squeezing splinters, or they could be mangles, painfully scraping back and wringing out your hair after it had been washed — or, if she was comforting you, they could be as soft and soothing as a lullaby.

★　★　★

The voyage home on a troopship called *Monarch of Bermuda* took just under three weeks and we children were bored and seasick — that smell of vomit combined with engine oil and stale cooking on an old boat turns my stomach to this day — but we must have felt OK occasionally because we got into serious trouble for eating all the chocolate in the emergency ration kits that we had to carry with us at all times, along with our life jackets, in case the ship was torpedoed. We were sent to Sunday School — anything to fill in the hours, I suppose — which we liked because the teacher illustrated Bible stories by moving cut-out felt figures around on a felt board. And there was a huge thrill when our ship passed through the Suez Canal and stopped at Port Said where it was invaded by rather scary conjurors called Gully Gully Men, who did magic tricks which mostly involved producing baby chicks out of your ears or the back of your neck.

As we neared Liverpool, our mother's excitement at the thought of her reunion with David (and with her own parents) had infected us all, but life has a way of kicking you in the teeth at moments like these, and our homecoming was a cruel, crushing disappointment. Because the war with Japan was still in full swing then, no one was allowed to mention the names of ships, or dates and times of sailings, for fear of encouraging torpedo attacks. Our parents had had to communicate our arrival details to the family in England in some sort of code, and the code they chose had to do with Grandpa's birthday: we were arriving six days after it or three days before it, something like that. I don't know what went wrong but somehow our relatives failed to decipher the message correctly and that meant there were no beaming faces and arms stretched out to welcome Mum and us girls at the docks in Liverpool: no one was there at all. Miserably, we caught the train to Liverpool Street station in London, but there was no one there either. We crossed London to Waterloo to catch the train to Fleet (where my grandparents and David lived) — there was no one at Waterloo, and worst of all, no one at Fleet station when we arrived, and no one at home when we got there except for our slightly bemused grandfather and our four-year-old cousin Simon. All the other relatives had gone to meet us at the wrong time in Liverpool, so poor Mum had to wait several more long hours before the welcoming party of David and our grandmother and aunt and cousins turned up, just as tired and frustrated as we were.

★ ★ ★

We spent eighteen months in England living with our grandparents in their Edwardian redbrick house in Fleet. It was called Landour and when I grew older I felt quite ashamed of this (as well as of our tubular metal gate which was made in the shape of a sunburst) because it was obviously Our Land backwards. I only discovered later that it was not that at all — Landour is a small town in India named long ago, presumably by Welsh ex-pats, after the town of Llanddowror. (But the gate remained a gate with a sunburst on it.)

My grandparents had spent most of their lives in India — he as a railway engineer — but they originally came from Ireland and I didn't know until recently that they made the decision to retire to Hampshire and not to Dublin because of Irish politics. Three of my four grandparents were Catholics, but my mother's father came from an Anglo-Irish Protestant family and during the Irish Troubles they were targeted — in fact his cousin's house in Dublin was burned to the ground. Grandpa decided to take no risks and settled in Fleet where there was a good bridge club. (Perhaps he was right to be fearful: when, in the Fifties, we went back to Ireland on holiday in a car with GB plates, we had clods of earth thrown at us.)

It was a sad household when we arrived because my Aunt Thea, who lived there too with her children, had lost her husband almost exactly one year before, in the war in Burma: he had been killed in the very last days of the Battle of Kohima, and our young cousins Jinny and Prue and Simon now had no father.

Everything about England was an unpleasant shock to us 'Indian' children with our funny accents and sallow faces: here at 'home' in just-post-war, still-rationed, grey, suffering Britain, our new relatives did not seem to be particularly thrilled to see us, and were quite strict. I was aware that they thought we were thoroughly spoiled, and what's more, unlike them, we had escaped the miseries of the war in England. I cried for India and for Ayah-Ma.

We especially dreaded the meals — in India we had eaten delicious rice and dhal, and vegetable curry, and something called egg cutlet (or a variation of it, vegetable cutlet — they both still exist in India), and we had tasty snacks like *pakoras*, and sugar cane to chew, and we feasted on papaya and passion fruit and lychees and guavas and Alphonso mangoes (we used to dry the hairy seeds in the sun to make dolls' heads: you scraped the fibres off one side of the mango seed and then drew a face on this bald bit, leaving the furry part to be the 'hair').

We were used to delectable Indian sweets made of boiled-down milk and flavoured with cardamom: *burfi*, *gulab jamun* or, different but equally delicious, *jalebi* (deep-fried spirals of crispy batter soaked in syrup) — all the stuff of impossible dreams in England where sugar, milk, butter, eggs and flour were rationed.

Dad once showed me a tapeworm cyst (cooked and dead) under the skin of some pork in our kitchen in India, but there was no friction at meals except one day when Dad imitated me grabbing the cheese biscuits off the tray when they were handed round, giving all of us a fright, especially Mario, our bearer who was holding the tray. If anything, we were told not to eat too much, not to be greedy (hence the lesson about not grabbing the biscuits). Dad used to tell us about someone called the Rajah of Marmdote (we never knew if he was real or made up) who had Eating Disease which meant he could not resist food. Knowing this, his subjects used to line his driveway as he passed by, all smacking their lips over delicious-looking snacks. 'Give me a bite of that,' the rajah would plead. 'Oh please let me taste — just a tiny mouthful, I beg you . . . ' But his subjects would hold the food away until he offered them huge bribes, and so they all grew rich and happy and the rajah grew very plump.

Now, here in England, there was nothing nice to eat because of the war and rationing, and our meals seemed to be meat that was gristle and fat, and fish with flabby white skin on one side and even worse flabby grey skin on the other, and we were told to eat it all up and not make a fuss, and certainly not leave anything on our plates. One dish is lodged in my memory: plaice fillets — flabby skin on — rolled and secured with a toothpick, in glutinous white sauce made with margarine and flavoured with Marmite. Simon missed an outing to London Zoo because he refused to eat his fish; he was made to sit in front of it for days, I seem to remember, but he never gave in. Tessa became a vegetarian as soon as she grew up.

The other horror was that in those days greens seemed to be full of caterpillars and slugs, and even though our mothers used to put the leaves to soak in the sink in salty water to get them out,

47

you could still find them dead in your food or, with salad, walking round your plate. Only the other day AW and I were talking about the awfulness of just-post-war meals; remembering tinned whale meat and greasy Spam fritters set us off thinking how lucky children are now with delicious junk food — oven chips, pizzas, burgers, fish fingers, ketchup, etc. — and with lettuce and broccoli sold in plastic bags with not a slug or maggot or caterpillar in sight.

In Fleet the concept of actually *looking forward* to a meal was beyond our imagining, though, to be fair, Tessa and I did love our aunt's 'porridge pudding' made of oats mixed with raw apple, raisins, sugar and milk. (I realise now that she'd invented *muesli* without knowing it.) And we liked being dosed with a tonic called Parrish's Food — it was pinky-red and slightly sharp to taste and you had to drink it with a straw (which seemed very sophisticated to us) because otherwise the iron in it stained your teeth black. Come to think of it, we were always being fed with 'tonics' in those days — slimy white stuff called Scott's Emulsion, as well as cod liver oil and malt; and grown-ups seem to have been obsessed by constipation as well, because we were always being asked if we'd done 'big jobs' as it was called then, which felt intrusive and embarrassing even at our young ages, and if we hadn't, we'd be dosed with Syrup of Figs. I never gave my own children any of these things.

When we got colds we were made to sit at the kitchen table with a towel over our heads, breathing up the steam from a bowl of hot water laced with Friar's Balsam, which was so boring and uncomfortable we dreaded it. A much cosier memory of being ill is of Mum beside the bed, vigorously shaking the thermometer down, then examining it, and shaking it down again before putting it under our tongues — I still think of this ritual as one of the most comforting of childhood: someone was in charge and would make you better. (Mercury thermometers gave us lots of other pleasure: if they broke you could pour the big drop of cold shiny mercury into a cup and play with it, breaking it into hundreds of tiny droplets which could then be made to join up into one again.)

* * *

After the skimpy outfits we'd worn in India, getting dressed in England seemed a huge effort, with knickers (two pairs: thin white ones under another, thicker, usually coloured, pair), vests, socks, shirts, skirts, jumpers, cardigans, overcoats/raincoats and scarves, plus Clarks sandals that had to be buckled. A girl called Renee was employed, part-time, to look after us and take us for walks but she used to arrange to meet her friends and would chatter to them for hours while we just stood there, cold and bored to death. We couldn't really complain, though, because our cousins were so much worse off than us, not having their father any more. And, in any case, overriding all the bad and sad things about England was the fact that we had our new family to play with: there were endless thrilling games of Kick-a-Peg (or Forty Forty as it seems to be known now), and I think I had more fun than perhaps at any time since, with Simon and Tessa, pretending that the small mats that were placed in front of the doors in our grandparents' hallway were ships — we each had one — and that the Edwardian tiled floor was a sea full of sharks. And we played Robin Hood — which was less fun for me as being a bit podgy I was always given the part of Friar Tuck while Simon was Robin, and Tessa (who was/is very pretty) was Maid Marian and got to wear the glittery sequin jacket from the dressing-up box. I ached to wear it but was never allowed to play Maid Marian. (Tessa confessed the other day that she still has it.) Tessa and I had never been friends with a boy before; oddly, though we were all very young and lived together in Landour, we were never bathed together or saw each other naked — I once bribed Simon to show me his willie, not in a rude way, but in the nature of scientific research.

We had two white mice which Tessa and I decided to keep in a doll's house we'd been lent to play with (I think Grandpa had made it for our cousins Jinny and Prue). Of course they instantly escaped and were never seen again. Granny was cross and said they would mate with their wild relatives and create a mouse problem.

We spent some of our leisure time (I suppose it was the equivalent of modern children playing computer games) listening to 'Teddy Bears' Picnic' and the story of Sparky and his magic piano on the gramophone. The Sparky story was particularly brilliant because it came on three 78 records which were stacked on to the spindle of the gramophone all together, and then, miraculously, dropped down on to the turntable in order, one by one, at which point the arm holding the needle swung over *all by itself* to play them. It seemed like the cutting edge of technology for us — well, I suppose it *was* the cutting edge of technology then. Incidentally, Sparky was a little boy whose piano suddenly came alive and played itself — all Sparky had to do was run his fingers over the keys and the piano would produce a perfect performance of whatever he had announced he would play. Only Sparky knew this secret, everyone else believed he was a child prodigy, and he became famous for his playing, but he also became spoiled and rude and unpleasant, until one terrible day — at Carnegie Hall, in the middle of a concert — the piano tells Sparky that it will no longer play for him and the frantic boy bashes the keys crying, 'Play, piano, play' . . . and it all turns out to have been a dream. I mention this because all through my career I have often thought of Sparky — whenever I have managed to write something that I am particularly pleased with, I wonder, secretly, if my typewriter/computer did it for me.

★　★　★

Our new-found seventeen-year-old brother David was dazzling: handsome and funny and sweet to us; we hero-worshipped him when he came home on holiday from boarding school. He'd built a wooden shack, Ivy Cottage it was called,

51

by the stream at the bottom of my grandparents' garden and we spent most of the time there, or in our rather taciturn grandfather's tool shed where he let us 'help' make jigsaws with his fretsaw. (Later, after we returned to India, Grandpa, most unexpectedly, sent us a series of thrilling stories he'd written about the adventures of a girl called Briditia — a combination of Brigid and Patricia, my sister Tessa's real name. They were illustrated by my cousins Jinny and Prue. I am always meaning to try and get them printed for my grandchildren.)

In the end we became fond of our aunt and our grandmother, who was a bit scatty — she once saw a group of her friends chatting away in the high street in Fleet. As she passed them, she smacked one of them on the bum, saying: 'Gossip! Gossip! Gossip!' The women turned round in surprise, and to her horror Granny saw they were total strangers.

★   ★   ★

Not long ago, Fleet was nominated as a) one of the best places to live in Britain and b) the town where more sex toys are sold than anywhere else — are a) and b) related? one wonders. In our day, presumably because of its nearness to Aldershot — which used to be known as 'Home of the British Army' — Fleet was stuffed with retired Indian Army families like ours who, thankfully, wouldn't have known a sex toy from a plate of kedgeree — though, to be fair, I don't think the toys had yet been invented in the 1940s.

The only notable thing about Fleet then was that there was a genuine *patisserie* shop, run by a real Frenchwoman called Madame Max (how/why/when did she come to dreary old Fleet? I wish I knew her story). Bread rationing in England was introduced while we were there, in 1946, and you could only buy the meagre amounts of bread (or cakes, I suppose) that you had coupons for in your ration book; when he was at home Granny used to send David up to Madame Max pretending he'd lost the coupons to try and wheedle some extra treats — he was always sent back empty-handed.

The awesome thing — the *only* thing, really — we knew about Grandpa's long life in India as a railway engineer, before he came 'home' to Fleet, was that one day at work out in the countryside he was attacked by a leopard: it leapt on him as he walked through some long grass, sank its claws into his shoulders and used him as a springboard to launch itself on to the man behind him. Grandpa could never lift his arms up very high as a result of his injuries, but, so the story went, the other man died of his.

All I ever knew about Granny's life in India was that she taught her cook how to make a delicious dish of fish with finely sliced vegetables wrapped in parcels of greaseproof paper and baked in the oven. The cook seemed to grasp the idea and Granny decided to serve this at some posh dinner she was giving. To her horror, when the *papillotes* were brought in on a big platter she saw that the cook had taken a short cut — instead of snipping out squares of greaseproof paper as she had shown him, he had used sheets of lavatory paper (which was a bit like greaseproof in those days) and each little parcel had BRONCO stamped on it somewhere.

★ ★ ★

I promised my father before he died that (with an exception which I will explain later) I wouldn't read his letters to my mother, but I never promised not to read Mum's to him, and so, recently, I dipped into the ones she wrote at this time — from mid-1945 to autumn 1946 — and learned of her fears for him, first in the Middle East (Lebanon, Syria and Palestine) and then back in India, and her concerns about us returning there, and her worries about money, and what would happen to us if and when we left India and returned to England for ever . . . I also discovered that Tessa and I were sent to dancing classes in Fleet, because in one letter Mum, who'd watched a lesson while waiting to take us home, writes, 'Oh dear, Brigid is not exactly graceful, but you do have to give her full marks for trying, bless her.'

★ ★ ★

As I explained earlier, Tessa and I had never been to school, but now, after the best part of a year and a half in Fleet with our grandparents, we were going back to India, and a governess had been hired to come with us. Moira, poor Moira, was to be left behind to go to boarding

54

school; and David, who had already been separated from his family for so long, was to go to Sandhurst.

The governess was called Miss Waller, which immediately became Swaller, and we came to love her indomitable, jolly-hockey-sticks, isn't-life-a-huge-adventure character dearly. I can't think of a single academic thing she taught us, but I did learn that one should always carry a book to read in case you get held up somewhere with nothing to do, plus a cardigan in case the weather changes, and you should try to keep a small notebook and pencil handy, as well as something to eat and drink in an emergency. These lessons have proved invaluable. I don't mean to be smug, but our children were always the good ones on planes when they were small, thanks to my Swaller-inspired bag of activities, books, biscuits and drinks.

# 3

We returned to a turbulent India, but, as children, we were sheltered and our early days back in the country seemed peaceable, and I was happy to be there and not at all homesick for England. We lived for a short time in a boarding house or small hotel in a military town called Secunderabad which is next to Hyderabad in the centre of India. I don't know why we were staying in a hotel, we had never lived in one before, but perhaps Brightlands, the house in Bolton Road whose address I wrote in every book, was being painted or cleaned up for us. Outside the hotel was a pile of builders' sand and, when we were not having lessons or creating pompoms or doing French knitting with Swaller (her passion for making things never left me), Tessa and I spent every day perfectly happily climbing over it, picking out tiny shells which we collected in matchboxes. We were in the boarding house/hotel for Christmas 1946, all of us feeling glum because we were not in our own home (wherever that was meant to be) and Dad was, as always, away, so it was just Mum and Swaller, Tessa and me and NO TREE. Mum cut a huge Christmas tree out of stiff paper and painted it green with coloured decorations and pinned it to the wall but it wasn't quite the same. Then, in the middle of our muted celebrations, there was a knock at the door and Dad appeared

— he was in uniform and had somehow managed to get away from whatever he was doing, to be with us for a few hours. It was thrilling.

Soon we moved to 219A Bolton Road in Secunderabad, Dad was with us at last, my grandmother came on a visit from England, and so did our glamorous young Aunt Joan who was on her way back to England from Australia where she had been a Wren radiographer in the war (rumour had it that she had bunked off without being properly discharged so could be arrested for desertion at any time). Aunt Joan was much younger than Mum, and she had boyfriends and sang us 'Lili Marlene' and 'Don't Fence Me In' and we saw her as Glamour personified.

Tessa and I had our lessons with Swaller and played in the fountain in the garden (always on the alert for snakes), but the highlight of our days was going swimming at the Club where I spent weeks quivering on the sodden coir matting of the high diving board, plucking up courage to jump — luckily, the day I did, someone was there with a camera. I prided myself on being able to open my eyes underwater and one day I was asked to look for a gold earring which a wealthy young Indian woman had lost in the pool. I found it, and triumphantly presented it to her, and she gave me some sweets which was a bit disappointing as I had thought she would give me the earring — or some other jewel at least. I was always over-optimistic ... (Years later I found a diamond ring in a

57

flowerbed in our garden in England. It was man-sized and rather ugly but it became my most treasured possession — until there was some kind of crisis in the world and the priest in church told us we must give our most precious possession to charity; I gave the ring. My mother told her friend Eileen what I had done, and when Eileen died, she left me a beautiful Georgian diamond ring. It was stolen by my cleaning lady in London.)

These were happy days. In the early evenings we sat with Mum and Dad in cane chairs on the lawn, while they smoked cigarettes (which came in tins in India, not packets) and had whiskies and sodas, and we'd beg them to let us have a mynah bird or a monkey. We pleaded so hard that in the end they did agree that a monkey could be brought to meet us to see how we all got on, but it didn't seem to like Tessa, so it was taken away again. One evening they had friends for drinks and when I announced that there had been a lady making cow-dung pats in our garden that day, everyone burst out laughing and I didn't know why. I was puzzled and slightly hurt about this for years until I grew up and realised that everyone was obsessed by class in those days, and so the idea of a 'lady' making cow-dung pats was hilarious to them.

Mum always had some project in hand: painting the flowering trees of India, embroidering a map of her journey home by bus, smocking cotton dresses for us which meant her ironing on the transfers of dots you had to follow for this. She and Dad were full of curiosity and there was nothing they liked more than an outing. Whenever they were together, sooner or later there would be expeditions to temples, forts or ruins of some sort. We loved the excitement of the trips — setting out in the cool of early dawn when the sky was the palest blue — but the cultural side of them was rather wasted on Tessa and me. All I can remember of Golconda, near Hyderabad, one of the greatest fortresses in India, was whining about the long walk up the hill to get to it, and at the famous caves of Ellora and Ajanta, while the grown-ups looked reverently at the carvings and paintings illuminated by light reflected into the dark interiors by a man holding a mirror, Tessa and I spent the whole time quarrelling and being shouted at by Dad.

One excursion ended with horror: we had gone to look at the dam at Pocharam where a huge reservoir supplied (probably still supplies) the water for the town of Pune. We walked along the mighty dam and looked down, and far below we saw that some men were splashing about in the water, while people on the bank were running up and down, shouting and gesticulating. Dad started bellowing down instructions. At first we thought the flap was because swimming there was not allowed, but then we understood what was happening — the men were caught in a current and were being sucked towards a giant pipe, presumably the one that took the water to the town. We were hurried away and later told they had been saved, but from what Tessa and I remember we are not convinced that was true.

Soon the profound political changes that were taking place in India began touching even us children's lives though of course we didn't understand what was making everyone so worried and uneasy.

The British prime minister, Clement Atlee, had announced in February 1947 (a couple of months after we'd got back there) that India was to become independent of the British who had ruled it for some two hundred years. Lord Mountbatten, a British statesman with connections to the royal family, was appointed Viceroy of India with the task of organising Indian independence, and, as well, implementing a controversial plan: the partition of India into two countries, a new one called Pakistan to be a homeland for Muslims, alongside a slightly reduced India.

In June that year Mountbatten announced that all these extraordinary changes would be achieved by mid-August: that on 14 August 1947, Pakistan would celebrate its creation and independence, while the next day, 15 August, the new India would celebrate its own autonomy. This meant that there were *only two months* in which to work out where to draw the border — nearly 2,000 miles long — between India and Pakistan; two months to prepare for a massive exchange of populations when twelve *million* men, women and children would move countries: Muslims from India to the newly formed Pakistan; and Hindus, living in what was about to become Pakistan, to India. There were only two months for the British to hand over the vast subcontinent and prepare for their departure; two months to reorganise every single aspect of the administration of India, from the government departments, to the railways, to the police and the army.

For Tessa and me, most of this was way over our heads, though we knew about Indian independence because '*Jai Hind!*' ('Victory to India!') was the catchword of the day: it was '*Jai Hind!*' when you met people, or passed them in the road; '*Jai Hind!*' on flags, on posters, in graffiti, on matchbox labels — and we were as excited about Indians getting their independence as they were. But every day, it seemed, events took place that upset my parents: one afternoon my father came home and told my mother that the Indian Army, as well as the Indian police force, were to be divided, with Muslim soldiers and policemen going to Pakistan and Hindus staying in India. My mother was appalled and bewildered; she didn't believe such a thing was possible: the world she was so familiar with was falling apart.

The old India hands — people like my parents who had been born there and lived there all their lives — were shocked at the very short amount of time Mountbatten had allocated to achieving the handover of power and a peaceful division of the country. They considered him spoilt and privileged, overambitious and lacking in knowledge about India, making fateful decisions without any real experience of the place. Dad referred to him as the Fairy Prince, and a joke undermining Lady Mountbatten went the rounds: in India Girl Guides were called Girl Guides, but for obvious reasons, the Brownies were called Bluebirds. The story was that Lady Mountbatten had opened a Guides rally, absent-mindedly saying: 'It is wonderful to be with all of you young Guides and little Blackbirds today.' I have no idea if this is true or not.

My parents and their friends talked about the traumatic events that were happening all around us, and snippets of their conversations seared into my mind — for instance, in 1947 when two thousand tribesmen invaded Kashmir from Pakistan, I overheard the grown-ups discussing how, on their way into the valley, the marauders had raided a convent in Baramulla where they had raped the nuns and then pulled any gold teeth out of their mouths. I was utterly appalled: I didn't know what rape meant, but the idea of someone's teeth being pulled out with pliers was the worst thing imaginable, and it could obviously happen even to a white person like us, and even to a NUN if she were in the wrong place — what worried me was, were we in the wrong place?

By then our cosy family life in Secunderabad had come to an end because Dad had gone to serve with the Punjab Boundary Force, and the rest of us — Mum, Aunt Joan, Swaller, Tessa and me — were staying with Mum's Uncle George (always known as U.G.), a retired indigo planter who lived in a house called The Homestead in

Kotagiri, a village in the Nilgiri Hills. Tessa and I liked it there; we kept out of his way because we were a bit scared of him, but he had two little dogs that we loved, and a passion-fruit vine growing over the front doorway from which we could help ourselves to the fruit at any time (passion fruit is my whole childhood in one taste). Once he told us a frightening story about friends of his who were out in an open horse-drawn trap just up the road from his house, when a leopard sprang right across it — from one side of the road to the other — snatching up their dachshund in its claws as it passed. It was a thrilling tale, but it left Tessa and me with a new thing to worry about that we hadn't thought of before: to the fear of snakes and tooth-pulling tribesmen from Pakistan we now had to add leopards — which apparently teemed in the rather-too-close forest around The Homestead. We were reading *The Jungle Book* at that time and it was completely alive to us because Mowgli's world, with Bagheera his leopard friend, Hathi the elephant and Shere Khan the tiger, was at the end of our garden; it was territory we knew — almost an extension of our own lives. The Little Black Sambo books were our other favourites: apart from Kipling's, they were the only children's stories in English that were relevant to us growing up in India, the only ones we could identify with — their heroes and heroines being Indian children, similar to the ones we saw every day, surviving terrifying adventures involving snakes, tigers, muggers (Indian crocodiles), mongooses, monkeys, bazaars, unkind grown-ups and big earthenware pots called *chat-ties* exactly like the ones which held water in our own kitchen. We didn't particularly notice that the children in the stories were black and of course we didn't know then that Sambo was a pejorative word.

Helen Bannerman, the author of these now-controversial books, became a bit of a hero to me later in life when I discovered a little about her. She was born in Edinburgh in the middle of the nineteenth century when women were not yet permitted to attend university in Scotland, but could study and take examinations exter-nally; in this way she became one of the very first women to gain an LLA (Lady Literate in the Arts) degree. She married a doctor in the Indian Medical Service and spent thirty years with him in India, helping local people, and when their four children were born, she wrote the books for them. She had long since died by the time the backlash over Little Black Sambo began years ago, but her son, Robert, wrote in a letter to *The Times*, 'My mother would not have published the book had she dreamt for a moment that even one small boy would have been made unhappy . . . ' Her grandson is the distinguished physicist Sir Tom Kibble, who is one of the co-discoverers of the Higgs boson.

When we returned to England, Little Black Sambo and his fellow characters remained precious because they reminded us of India, but the books that then resonated with us were *The Secret Garden* and *A Little Princess* by Frances Hodgson Burnett, because they were about

Indian-born girls being unhappy back in their own country. Later, like every other teenager, I imagine (did *any* girls want to be Meg or Amy?), I identified with Jo in *Little Women* because she was the odd one out, though it annoyed me for ages that she married the Professor and not Laurie — but then I fell in love with *The Scarlet Pimpernel* so I didn't really care any more.

★   ★   ★

From grown-ups' conversations we gathered that Dad, far away in Punjab, was not particularly happy, but we had no real idea of what he was doing; it was only after we grew up that he ever spoke to us about it, or that we learned of the horrors which came with the partition of India — and it was only after our parents had died that Tessa found the big envelope of letters that Dad wrote to Mum at this grim time (and which I never promised not to read because we didn't know they existed). But the unbelievably terrible events he witnessed then, and his powerlessness to improve the situation, changed him — and it altered the course of our lives — so I will try and explain.

By Indian Independence Day, with some exceptions (including Dad), the 60,000 British soldiers who had served in the army in India had either left, or were confined to barracks as they prepared to leave, while the remaining bulk of the Indian Army was divided up (as I explained earlier), with Hindu soldiers staying put and their Muslim counterparts leaving to form the

65

new Pakistan Army. The same thing happened with the Indian police force: British members were sent home to England while the rest of the force was split, with the Muslims going off to Pakistan. All this created a huge vacuum in India: there was no strong, neutral peacekeeping authority left to control the new border between India and Pakistan (which ran alongside the Sikh heartland) as millions of people with two fundamentally different religions began to cross it in opposite directions. And to add to the tension, the actual path of the border line itself was not announced until two days *after* Independence so those who lived along it did not know, literally, whether they belonged to India or Pakistan.

Realising there might be problems ahead, Mountbatten set up the Punjab Boundary Force of about 17,000 soldiers and local police, which came into being two weeks or so before Independence, to try to keep the peace in this explosive situation — but there were not enough men or resources allocated (members of the PBF, as it was known, called themselves the Poor Bloody Fools), and it could not do the job expected of it. Hindus, particularly the Sikhs, whose territory the Muslim refugees had to cross to reach Pakistan, started attacking and slaughtering departing Muslims and Muslims in Pakistan did vice versa. What made it infinitely worse was that, though most of the population had no weapons, the Sikhs were armed with three-foot-long swords called *kirpans* which could not be taken from them as they are a

66

religious symbol. The ensuing massacres were known as the Bloodbath: it is believed that a million people died.

My father arrived in the Punjab on 10 August 1947 to take up his peacekeeping duties for Lahore district, plus Ferozepur and Montgomery areas — all places that did not yet know whether they would be in India or Pakistan when the border was announced. He wrote to Mum on 13 August telling her how, on his first day, he had come upon the dead bodies of forty Muslim men, women and children lying in the road, slaughtered by Sikhs, and that 'panic reigns everywhere'. From then on he wrote to her daily and in each new letter the horrors mounted — though he was at the same time clearly trying to protect her from the more terrible details.

Dad hoped that things would improve when the border was defined — 'We are longing for the Boundary to be announced and get it over ... ' — but, if anything, when that happened it made the situation worse. In his own areas, Lahore district was divided between India and Pakistan; Ferozepur went to India (though 50 per cent of its inhabitants were Muslims who began to move out) and Montgomery went to Pakistan, though it had a similarly huge Hindu population who also began to move, in the opposite direction.

Now more and more refugees — hundreds of thousands — were on the road. 'I have about 8 lacks [800,000] refugees, both Muslim and Sikh/Hindu, passing through my districts and as they are going against each other there is grave

67

danger of mass encounters en route,' Dad wrote. 'Our troops are fully extended and going all out to make sure this mass migration is coloured with as little blood as possible, yet a heavy toll is taken every time . . . You see, columns of a lack [100,000] are at least 8 miles long and usually one can spare only one platoon to do the job of escorting them. Crops, grass, etc are good cover, right up to the road, and the murderers come in with their swords and spears and do their killing before escort troops can come up . . .

'You cannot realise what it looks like, seeing thousands of people go through here. Men, women and children, all with bundles or *charpoys*, bullock carts laden sky-high, tongas, handcarts, barrows, camels, buffaloes, cattle, goats, sheep, dogs, all miserable, all heavily laden, all with some tale of woe, all with very little to look forward to, most of them having left all or most of their most valuable possessions, human, animal or property, in some robber's or murderer's hands. My darling, I am glad you don't know what these poor people go through . . . my heart bleeds for them.'

A day or two later Dad wrote, 'I have never felt the animosity between Muslims and Sikhs more in all my service in India . . . ' and he went on to lament the fast-growing communal hatred — particularly of the Sikhs for the Muslims — as being like 'some foul loathsome disease . . . the lust to kill and burn, to destroy members of the hated other side and all they possess, be they the most innocent babes or harmless women. I shan't go into what happens every day, everywhere, but I think the saddest thing are abductions of women — or they kill them or slash their breasts and kill their babies . . . It's a Hitlerian campaign to eliminate as many child-bearers of the other side as possible. A lot of this I have not wanted to tell you before . . . '

Every day Dad's litany of death and misery continues: 'The papers are quiet about it all, but there is butchery, arson, murder, rape and theft on a large scale of everything conceivable going on in the Punjab now — chiefly done by Sikhs. It never lets up . . . they have begun to produce implements of all kinds, pitchforks, spears, lances, daggers, swords, pistols, revolvers, rifles, shotguns, automatic weapons and grenades.

'Firing a village is a normal occurrence like having breakfast, murder is like having a cigarette, and on the long trails to the main roads, you see everything from headless corpses and maimed women and butchered children to smouldering bullock carts and other property, marking the way . . . I tell you, darling, it is just sheer hell, and I have never conceived of such sufferings as I have witnessed . . . I don't think there is a parallel in history of two communities as numerous as these two (Muslims and Hindus) just going for each other hammer and tongs . . . We must hurry up and leave this country . . . The misery just makes one feel devastated and one's thoughts are of God and one's prayers are for mercy to suffering mankind.'

At one point, Dad writes that the refugees all carried bedding — light quilts known as *razais* in India — which they let fall when attacked or collapsing from hunger, exhaustion or illness, so that in places the whole landscape was patterned with these colourful cotton bedcovers trodden into the dust, or later, the mud. Of all the horrors Dad describes, somehow the image of those thousands of abandoned quilts — and what they represent — is the one that I cannot shake from my mind.

Dad saw the notorious refugee trains — both Muslim and Hindu — which arrived at their destinations full of dead passengers; he saw camps where there was almost nothing to sustain the refugees and where many hundreds of dead were left behind each time a group moved on; he saw the suffering increase a hundred times over when September rains caused floods and even more chaos and death — but the betrayal by the rajah of a Sikh state called Faridkot is the event that seems to have disturbed him most; it is the one he talked about to Tessa and me. In particular he mentioned to us several times seeing a baby that had had its throat cut but was still alive, trying to crawl into shade — it obviously haunted him, but we never understood why this child affected him more than all the hundreds of others.

On 27 August Dad wrote that he had been to see the Rajah of Faridkot to discuss, and organise, the orderly departure of the 60–70,000-strong Muslim community in his state. Dad had not been impressed by the rajah: 'He is a child in many ways. He giggles, talks about his armoured cars . . . Two hours of him was enough.' But he had come to an agreement with him that he must hold the refugees for ten days until everything was ready for them, and 'that we expected the roads and railway not to be molested . . . all in a most diplomatic way of course'.

The rajah had agreed the route that the refugees would take out of his state: they would travel towards the north gate where Dad would have a battalion standing by to protect them once they crossed the border (the Punjab Boundary Force was not allowed to operate within the independent Sikh states), but when the time came the rajah sent them out on a different road, west, to the neighbouring state of Muktsar, where there was no protection.

Dad seems to have discovered this on what he described as his worst day. He was touring the area with Colonel Sant Singh, an Indian officer, when in Muktsar they came upon a refugee column, miles long, that had been attacked by Sikhs hiding in the elephant grass at the side of the road. 'I saw and counted 300 murdered men, women and children and about the same number of wounded, mostly so badly cut across the neck that the head wobbled; and the most brutal attacks on women and children,' he wrote on 7 September. 'We picked up about twenty children from two weeks old to about two years who had had parents and relatives blotted out. I cannot tell what a massacre it was . . . '

'But worse was to come. In Faridkot State near our border we met the sick, injured, aged, maimed, dead, who could not move. There were 140 women in labour, many had miscarriages;

babies sucking breasts of their dead mothers, many corpses — for cholera had broken out. Darling, I hope never to see such poor exhausted people suffer so much ever again . . . I am afraid it affects me very much.'

It is not absolutely clear that the dead and wounded Dad saw in Muktsar were from Faridkot, but it seems so because, though he does not say what he did next in his letter to Mum, he told Tessa and me that he was so distraught and full of rage that he drove straight to Faridkot and stormed into the rajah's palace with his revolver in his hand, intending to shoot him — but the rajah pleaded for his life and said he had only allowed his people to attack the refugees because they thought he was pro-Muslim and he had to prove he wasn't.

★  ★  ★

Shortly after the Faridkot affair, Dad reported that a colleague, Brigadier Wheeler, had resigned. 'He said he could not be a party to the policy of wholesale murder of Muslims by India . . . General Pete Rees (the commander of the PBF) asked me what my feelings were and I said: 'As long as I could help relieve the suffering of these unfortunates I would stay and do my best . . . '' By now, though, Dad too had abandoned any idea of staying on in India or Pakistan and was planning to leave himself: 'The PBF experience has made practically every single British officer cancel any option he may have made to serve on . . . '

The Punjab Boundary Force only existed for about a month — during which time, Dad wrote, a BBC reporter visited the region and, having seen what the force was required to do and the area they had to cover, commented that General Rees should have had at his disposal five times the number of troops he'd been allocated. At midnight on 31 August, the PBF, which had worked neutrally on both sides of the border, was disbanded, and instead India and Pakistan assumed responsibility for the security of their own refugees.

Dad continued his work more or less seamlessly, as he had told General Rees he would, but now under the authority of the Indian Governor of East Punjab. Every day the situation worsened as the whole region suffered unprecedented rain-fall: rivers burst their banks, roads were swept away, refugee camps inundated. 'I could not sleep last night thinking of the plight of *lacks* (hundreds of thousands) of refugees out in the open without fires to cook food, flooded out . . . God have mercy on them: they are suffering terribly. We have 80,000 here in Jullundur and babies etc, the old etc.'

On 22 September three new train massacres took place — two of Muslim passengers, one of non-Muslims — and 300 women and children were abducted from one of the Muslim trains. Dad wrote severely to Mum, who was desperate to be with him and had obviously made the suggestion she should bring us all up, 'For all our sakes don't be foolish . . . my earnest advice to you is STAY PUT. It is just asking for trouble,

73

five women and girls travelling together by rail, unescorted. However much I'd love you to be here I'd rather you delayed your arrival . . . '

Like many others, Dad worried that all India and Pakistan would explode when the refugees from both sides finally reached their destinations and told their appalling stories. 'Has U.G. got a gun/revolver?' he asked in the same letter. 'Tell him, without the servants noticing it, to keep it safe and handy . . . '

Mum listened to the advice not to travel; she did not move us and, mercifully, all India did not blow up as people had feared, and two months later, towards the end of the year, by which time most of the millions of refugees had either reached their new homelands or been murdered or abducted, Dad was no longer needed in East Punjab and rejoined us all in Kotagiri.

By now his decision not to stay on with the Indian Army (or with the Pakistan Army which had also approached him) was definite. We were going home, but first Dad had one last posting, as Poona Sub-Area Commander. I don't know why he took this on — perhaps it was a question of having to serve out notice?

Our farewell to the Nilgiri Hills was, to me, the most thrilling adventure ever: an elephant ride through the jungle at night. Tessa was considered too young to go, so she was sent off to stay with her friend Poochie. (After that, whenever you questioned some extraordinary and unlikely claim made by Tessa — e.g., 'When did you ride on a hippopotamus?' — she would say smugly, 'I did it at Poochie's house.')

I was included on the safari, though, and was scared stiff but bursting with excitement. Our elephants (we were on three, going single file) made their way through the forest just as dawn was breaking; no one spoke, but the *mahouts* guiding the great animals silently indicated where we should look, and we saw wild elephants, monkeys, deer, bison and wild boar. I sometimes wonder now if I dreamed the whole thing.

★   ★   ★

In Poona, Dad had the temporary rank of major-general and we lived in Flagstaff House, a low two-storey colonial building with bedrooms off a long veranda on the first floor. It was next door to an identical house which belonged to the senior general (in charge of the whole Indian Southern Command) and there, one shocking night, he was stabbed by an intruder. Tessa and I were woken up by shouting and running and confusion. Then next day, secretly thrilled, we crept into the garden when no one was looking to see the general's blood on the gate and on the path where he had collapsed in pursuit of his attacker. He survived, which was quite disappointing to us children actually, and it turned out his assailant was not some gallant Indian freedom fighter, but his gardener — which in a way is more interesting: what could have happened between the two of them that incited the gardener to risk everything to kill his employer? Or perhaps the gardener *was* a freedom fighter . . . we never discovered.

We were in our house in Poona on 30 January 1948 when the news came that Mahatma Gandhi had been murdered in Delhi. (Dad was always baffled as to how this information could have travelled so fast because Gandhi's death was not announced on the radio for some time after it happened.) We overheard Dad telling Mum that the general had just said, 'If Gandhi has been killed by a Britisher, we will all be dead by suppertime, and if he's been killed by someone from Poona, this city is going to go up in flames.'

We didn't have to wait very long to hear our fate — an hour or so; I was scared, but not THAT scared; perhaps I just couldn't imagine it. Luckily for us, Gandhi had not been killed by a Britisher, but he *had* been killed by someone from Poona, and that evening the city did go up in flames. Dad drove through it all in an armoured car, and came across Swaller bicycling casually along amidst the uproar, and sent her home.

A month later, on 28 February, Swaller and Tessa and I were taken by Mum and Dad to the Farewell to British Troops parade in Bombay: the departure of the very last British soldiers from India. We found the programme for the event among Dad's things after he died; the introduction says: 'In September 1754 two Companies of the 39th Foot, which later became the Dorsetshire Regiment, landed at Madras . . . the first soldiers of the British Regular Army to set foot in India. Today, nearly 200 years later

. . . the 1st Bn The Somerset Light Infantry, the last British battalion remaining in India, is leaving Bombay for England.'

This parade was the potent, visible end to the British Raj, and though I was only eight years old, I was aware that we were watching history, and that everyone around me was feeling emotional as we saw the last British soldiers march off the parade ground, through the Gateway of India, and straight on to launches that took them to their ship — but that didn't stop me eating the rice grains that had been stuck on my forehead (and on everyone else's) as a ceremonial gesture on arrival, and getting into trouble with Dad for disrespect.

★　★　★

Our final move in India was from Flagstaff House in Poona to Colaba transit camp in Bombay to wait for the ship that was to take us home for ever and ever. When we had returned to England in 1945, our transit camp had been Deolali — the place in which, over the years, so many British soldiers went mad from boredom, or heat, or venereal disease, that 'doolally' became another word for crazy in English. I got muddled about these camps and when, later, I went to school in England I shocked my teachers by telling them I had lived in two different *concentration* camps, rather than transit camps.

There must have been some kind of public pool or tank at Colaba because I was bullied by a much older English boy who ducked me and held me underwater until I thought I would drown. I was terrified of him but too scared to tell anyone. And then — I can't imagine how it ever came into our conversation — I mentioned to him that I had eaten an acorn when I'd been in England, and he said, 'You know what that means, don't you? Any child who eats an acorn will die before they are twelve.' I worried about this for four years, only really relaxing when I was twelve and one day old.

I have no idea how long we had to wait in Colaba for our ship home, and did we have our servants and their families with us there, or did they come specially to say goodbye at the end? I know they were on the dockside waving and crying — just as we were — when our ship sailed away from Bombay because we looked back on this later, with anguish. My father, who was always short of money, had most unusually made 'an investment' before we left India: he bought Moira and Tessa and me each a thick gold bracelet that was to be our inheritance (almost everything else our family owned had to be left behind in India — and Dad's parents' home in Burma had been burned down by the Japanese Army). These were packed away in one of our NOT WANTED ON VOYAGE trunks and it was only when they were unpacked in Fleet that Dad discovered the bracelets had disappeared. Apparently it would have been almost impossible for them to have been stolen on the ship, so we could only suppose that one, or maybe all, of those weeping figures on the dockside, getting smaller and smaller as our ship moved away, was actually secretly pleased at our departure. It was almost the worst thing about our leaving India.

* * *

No one ever feels any sympathy for those who are dispossessed of other people's possessions, i.e., the men and women who lived and served in the colonies and who had to go home when Independence came, whether it was from India, Indonesia, Algeria, West Africa or somewhere else. But I do, because I remember the heartache and the homesickness for the land we'd left. After five generations or more of my family's life and service in India, the only thing to show for it all now, in our daughters' lives, are a couple of Hindi words that have taken hold: *nanga panga*, meaning naked, and *kutchcha* for unfinished or shoddy, and the lullaby that Ayah-Ma used to sing to me that I in turn sang to my girls when they were babies, and that they now sing to their children. But I can still count to ten and recite 'Little Miss Muffet' in Hindustani (after a fashion), and remember words for things that were part of life when I was a child but have become obsolete now, such as *chilamchee*, for a travelling shaving kit with bowl, or *chaplee* for sandals which had a wrapover front, and whenever I taste passion fruit or hear crows cawing or the sound of sweeping, I am transported back to heat and sun and happy days.

I can't defend the British Raj in India. But I know my parents — good, honest, kind people who, as far as I could tell, always did their duty as they saw it — loved the place and thought about it until the day they died. When Dad was in his eighties, he and my mother, who was suffering from Alzheimer's disease by then, were invited to lunch with a group of AW's and my friends, among them a Kashmiri, Afzal, who is dear to us. Somehow, while we were all admiring the garden, Afzal came across Mum wandering around on her own looking for the loo and he helped her find and use it. Dad was touched and appreciative, and on the way home in the car he said, 'You cannot imagine how envious I am of you having close Indian friends; in my day it was not really possible,' and he began to cry, and I wept too for those lost friendships and the cruel artificial barriers erected by time and place, and power and history.

And I will be forever grateful for my eventful, scary, loving, warm, colourful childhood in India.

# 4

I have to hand it to my parents — they returned from life in Flagstaff House, Poona, with Dad as an acting-general and servants waiting on them hand and foot, to live in our grandparents' house in Fleet once again. Last time we'd stayed there, Dad had been in the Indian Army, but now it was 1948, he had no job and there were none available — the demobbed soldiers of the British wartime army had scooped up most of them, and the Brits who returned from India the year before us had got the rest. The only work my father could find was as eighth cowman on a farm. (One of his friends, an ex-admiral, became a lavatory attendant at Waterloo station.) I never really heard Mum and Dad grumble or complain or look back to the Good Old Days; Mum, especially, was homesick for India (she was not burdened with the terrible memories that haunted Dad), but they launched themselves into their new lives. Dad would set off for the farm on his second-hand motorbike at crack of dawn every morning in time for milking; it was tough for a middle-aged man, he lost weight and started getting boils, but Dad believed in getting on with things — we were brought up with his advice for life ringing in our ears (though why it was always said in French has been a perpetual mystery to me): '*Il faut saisir les occasions quand elles se présentent*', which basically means seize the day (it's the reason Tessa and I found ourselves in a helicopter in the Vietnam War, but I'll come to that later). Dad's other rule in life was Never Take No for an Answer — which, put together with his great charm, meant that shops were persuaded to let us in if we'd arrived late and found them closing, we always seemed to find seats even if the cinema or theatre was full, and he once talked our way into going behind the scenes at London Zoo to meet the chimps after their tea party.

Mum, who had never had to do anything in a kitchen before, tried to cook (she became good at it in the end) and she started a little kindergarten at home for a handful of kids so that Tessa could go to it. (When the children recited the alphabet they couldn't wait to shout out K is for KEENAN!)

I was sent to Miss Seed's, a small school in Aldershot where I was teacher's pet and had to make her Camp Coffee every morning (Camp Coffee was — is, because I believe it still exists — a kind of sweetened coffee syrup that you diluted with hot water or milk).

One of my fellow students from Fleet was an 'illegitimate baby', as the children of unmarried mothers were known then, called Anthony. We all felt sorry for him, and one day when he was crying because he'd lost his lunch box, I said, 'Tell your mum it was my fault.' Next day at the bus stop there was a furious, shouting mother demanding to be paid for a replacement, so I had to ask my parents for the money which got me into trouble with them too. That was the first time I realised that no good deed goes unpunished.

Mum used to tease me by saying 'Moira is the emerald in my crown, Tessa is the ruby and you are the little bit of glass that got in by mistake'; but she did it laughingly, and in such a way that I knew the little bit of glass was extremely precious to her — perhaps (I liked to think) even more precious than the others.

Something quite important to me happened at that time. For some reason I came home early from school one afternoon and no one heard me enter the house. I was approaching the kitchen and about to call out when I heard my mother and my aunt talking about me — 'It's a pity Brigid is such a desperately plain child,' one of them said, and the other agreed. I had no idea what 'plain' was, but it didn't sound good, so I crept back and re-entered making a lot of noise. Later I asked Moira what 'plain' meant. 'Oh it means something that's almost, but not quite ugly,' she said. I thought about this for years: Moira was attractive and clever and witty, Tessa was very pretty and funny, and I realised that I was going to have to do something — go for glamour, eccentricity, criminality, character, a career — *something*, so as not to end up at the bottom of the pile. There is a moment in her autobiography when the great beauty Lady Diana Cooper looks in the mirror, is disappointed by what she sees and says to herself, 'Now it's nap on personality.' I had the same sort of revelation, but aged nine.

Mum told us that, through Granny's family,

we were descended from Edward III, via his son John of Gaunt (the brother of the Black Prince). When I married AW I proudly informed him of this, but he once glimpsed the family tree at a reunion of cousins and became deeply sceptical. 'I have redrawn your family tree more accurately,' he said to me afterwards, and gave me a piece of paper which looked like this:

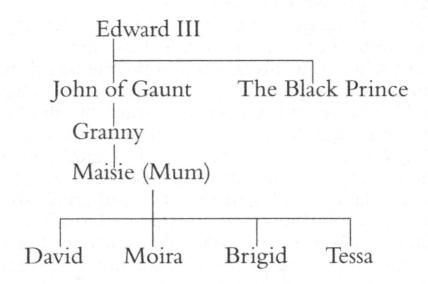

I laugh every time I think of it. In the meantime I have discovered that genealogists believe that 80 per cent of the English could be descended from Edward III because he had nine sons, so there wasn't really anything to boast about in the first place.

★   ★   ★

Dad was only eighth cowman on the farm but he had to take the cows up to London for the Dairy Show and watch over them all night in their pen or byre or whatever it was. His farmer-boss, a rich, landowning lady, used to introduce him to everyone proudly as her ex-general cowman, but quite soon Dad decided to train for a new career as a land agent. We stayed on in Fleet while he went away to the Royal Agricultural College in Cirencester to learn his new trade, and every night Mum and Tessa and I knelt and prayed for him to pass his exams: the family desperately needed him to be working and earning a salary. Dad did succeed, unlike most of his fellow students who were young landed gentry dashing to London in sports cars to have Fun in their spare time.

When we didn't have to pray for Dad any more, we prayed for the Russian people to be liberated from Communism. Britain and America were paranoid about the evils of Communism in the early Fifties and I caught the bug: Communism became my next anxiety. My dread was that it would take over England, and that Tessa and I would be dragged away from our beloved parents and put in some kind of Soviet youth retraining institution for ever — little did I know that boarding school would be more or less exactly that

★　★　★

Because of its British and Indian Army connections, the area around Fleet and Aldershot was a brilliant hunting ground for all kinds of exotic textiles and bits and bobs from the former colonies brought back from their travels by people like us who'd spent lifetimes overseas — and had now fallen on hard times, or were dead. Mum became a regular at Pearsons Auctions in Fleet where Persian rugs, Kashmir shawls and lacquerwork, and intricately carved Burmese chairs and tables all came up for sale; she had a brilliant eye but hardly ever had the money to buy the things she spotted. If only we'd known then what we know now: one of the greatest textile experts and collectors in the world, Michael Frances, told me once — at a beautiful exhibition of old Uzbek *suzanis* he had put on in Bond Street — that a number of his best pieces had been bought at Pearsons. He was smart: as a young man he had worked out that where there were people retired from Africa and India, there were likely to be interesting things in the local auction houses, and he was right.

Our house, Landour, was in the middle of Connaught Road, three blocks from the high street (an easy bike ride) where there was still Madame Max's *patisserie* shop, as well as a new toyshop staffed by a wacky young man who would hide behind the door and fire at people passing on the pavement with a peashooter. We nicknamed him Peter Pan. Later he went to work in the lingerie store which was quite off-putting — it's a bit creepy buying a bra from a man who has never grown up. Closer to our house was a greengrocer's where, bizarrely, they sold a few books alongside the potatoes. There I found the object of my dreams: a craft manual which told you how to make things out of lavatory rolls and cotton reels and straws and felt. Being a worthy kind of book, I thought my parents would buy it for me but they wouldn't; I had to hand over my pocket money for weeks to get it. Truth to tell, though I felt resentful at the time, my mother's words came true: I did value it more because I'd had to save for it.

Down one side of our typical redbrick suburban road there was Sergeant Mitten who lived in a bungalow with a flagpole in the garden; every night he would lower the Union Jack to the 'Last Post' played on a gramophone indoors near an open window, and every morning he raised it to 'Reveille'. Occasionally we used to lurk nearby and watch this ceremony. Beyond the sergeant was the canal where my father once staged a brilliant detective game: it started with a phone call at home one Sunday, allegedly from the police, saying they were looking for a missing person and could we children help. Then various clues led us to the canal towpath where, eventually, we found Dad lying in the under-growth with a knife smeared with ketchup on his chest — and his finger on his lips saying *ssssssh* to a group of traumatised walkers who had come across him before all of us had. I have just rung my sister Tessa because I suddenly wondered if this wasn't a completely false memory; she says she's almost, but not quite a hundred per cent, sure about the knife and the ketchup, but Dad in the undergrowth and the traumatised walkers is definitely true because she sometimes wonders how he hadn't been arrested before we arrived on the scene.

At the other end of the street, a four-minute

walk away, was the Catholic church, built like an ugly garrison church, in red brick. Because we were all Catholics (except Grandpa who was determinedly Protestant), this church figured large in our lives. The first priest we knew there turned out to be an abuser; he didn't abuse *us*, but we children were deeply suspicious of him — for one thing he often invited us to sit on his knee. The odd thing was that he was not in the mould of abusive priests, being English, an ex-vicar and a widower, but eventually he was found out and sent away, and Fleet was rewarded with a wonderful parish priest to make up for it: Canon Walsh, who remained a friend of the family for the rest of his life. (Twenty years on from this time in Fleet, he married AW and me, and twenty-eight years after *that* he married our daughter Hester and her husband.)

Religious services in the church in Fleet seemed to involve all of us children from Landour getting the giggles for one reason or another, and being helpless with suppressed laughter. Once it was because, late as usual, we entered a pew which was already full — we hadn't realised because they were standing up but when we all came to kneel it was bedlam — and once it was because an altar boy standing too close to the candleholder caught fire. No one understood what had happened; we were just flabbergasted to see the priest (it was the abusive one) suddenly turning on the boy and whacking him — not realising he was putting out flames.

★   ★   ★

As I have said before, for Tessa and me the main thrill of being in England was living in a house with our cousins. We shared a passion for jokes involving dressing up. One day, we all spent hours disguising our brother David as an Indian carpet seller — we painted his face brown, cut up hair to glue on his chin for stubble, tied a turban round his head, and he set off on his bicycle with Mum and Dad's rugs rolled up on the back to 'sell' them to a friend of our parents. She was in the garden when he cycled in through the gate, looked up and said, 'Hello David,' so that was a failure. A better effort was when we pretended that Simon was 'Mary', a friend of Jinny and Prue's from school. He wore one of their school uniforms and a school hat with someone's long-since-cut-off plaits pinned to the inside. He/she came to tea (we used to have proper tea every day, everyone sitting round a table with our parents or aunts or whoever was in the house) and we were all in stitches because my father was completely taken in. At one point Dad said, 'Mary, wouldn't you be more comfortable if you took off your hat?' and we fell off our chairs laughing and he was cross with us for being rude to our guest.

When Simon was about ten he painted an advertisement for Guinness — I think it was a picture of a man wrestling with a giant octopus on a beach with GUINNESS IS GOOD FOR YOU written underneath. Tessa and I were quite scathing of it, but he sent it off to Guinness and got back a boxful of goodies: little enamel pins of toucans (the Guinness logo) and foaming

Guinness glasses, plus posters and pencils. We were sick with jealousy and quickly painted our own advertisements and sent them off — but we received rather sharp letters in return, saying, basically, not to bother them.

David, a decade older than us, had a stack of ancient 78 records which we loved listening to: 'Buttons and Bows', 'Miss Otis Regrets', 'Bless You for Being an Angel' and 'So You Left Me for the Leader of a Swing Band'. (I always wanted to be asked on to *Desert Island Discs* so I could hear these songs again but I have just discovered that you can find them all on YouTube). We had no idea what a swing band was, and in fact half the time we misheard the words of the songs: there's a line in 'Miss Otis Regrets' which goes 'when the marb came and got her and dragged her from the jail'; I thought a 'marb' must be some sort of policeman in the US, and then I grew up and realised it was a mob in an American accent. AW thought Elvis was singing 'Pardon me, if I'm *second man*' in his song 'A Fool Such as I', instead of 'Pardon me, if I'm sentimental', and Mum once told us that when she was a child she thought the words in the Creed, 'suffered under Pontius Pilate', were 'shuffled him under a bunch of violets'.

In the evenings in Fleet we all gathered in the sitting room listening to the big brown radio which Grandpa first had to tune for what seemed like hours of EEEEEEE OOOOOOOO ZZZZZZZZ BRRRRRRR noises before we got to hear any words. (Cars that start first time and radios that work as soon as you switch them on

90

are luxuries that we didn't know about in the Fifties.)

Our grandfather sat next to the radio in case it needed a little tweak now and again, and played patience on a big wooden board that was greasy from use, while Mum and Granny and my aunts (our widowed Aunt Thea, and our young Aunt Joan who was living with us on and off then) and the rest of us all worked on some kind of knitting or embroidery or sewing. Very often, one of us young ones would be coerced into holding out our arms with a skein of wool stretched between them so that Granny or Mum or an aunt could wind the wool into a ball. For months on end I patiently did netting, which Grandpa had taught me, using string and a slat of wood. I was making an adult-sized hammock and when it was finished the whole family assembled to watch it being strung up between two trees in the garden. Then a boy who was staying with our cousins jumped into it — and went straight through the bottom . . . It was a crushing disappointment for me and the end of my enthusiasm for netting (but not other crafts).

The days seemed longer then, perhaps because they weren't gulped down by television and social media. We children did chores: helping Grandpa in the garden by picking up fallen leaves between two boards and putting them on the compost heap, or weeding the lawn with a neat little fork-like gadget that levered plantains and dandelions out by their roots; and in the house we laid the table and did the washing up which was even quite fun when we did it all together. Aunt Thea had just bought a set of unbreakable tumblers — a new invention. For some reason none of us knew the glasses were unbreakable apart from Jinny who decided to play a joke on us all; while we were busy drying up she stacked a whole lot of them together in a tall, wobbly tower and then called out, 'Look everyone,' and dropped them on the floor — where they broke into a million pieces. Everyone stared at Jinny as though she was mad ... she says she has felt guilty about it ever since. Why had the unbreakable glasses broken? We discovered later that they had shattered because they were wedged into each other.

After a while Dad got a job in the West Country, and we moved to Exmouth. Tessa and I went to a local convent where I got into trouble in Art for drawing women with bosoms, i.e., with a triangular bit sticking out of their fronts. This was considered 'rude' but as a child brought up in India, with all those improbable breasts on Hindu sculpture, I couldn't understand what I had done wrong. Almost the worst thing that happened in Exmouth was that Tessa and I got chicken-pox and had to stay in the school OVER THE EASTER HOLIDAYS. I don't know why we couldn't go home; Tessa thinks it might have been because our parents were doing something to our house — redecorating it? — and didn't want two sick children around. She has just reminded me that there was an up-side to having to stay on after term ended: we found a drawer full of the comic *School Friend*. At home, we had a subscription to *Girl* (which had a popular character called Lettice Leefe, the Greenest Girl in the School) and we loved it, but it was more educational and less racy than *School Friend* which was considered slightly naff — or, as they would have said in those days, 'common' — and wasn't allowed.

Other bad things that happened in Exmouth were that I fell downstairs on to a cactus on the landing and it took days to tweezer out all the prickles, and another, more serious, was that poor Mum was going through the menopause (though of course we didn't realise that at the time) which meant that she often had rapid heartbeat and believed she was dying, so the doctor would be called in the middle of the night — they still came out on house calls in those days — and we'd be woken by grown-ups whispering loudly and moving up and down stairs. It only occurs to me now that perhaps we had to stay at school when we got chickenpox because Mum couldn't cope?

Moira was the one who had to deal with all this; she was still living at home then, working as a secretary in Exeter. She earned so little, she told me later, that when she sent her suit to the dry-cleaner's she had to stay home until it was ready because she didn't have another outfit she could wear at the office.

After a year or so, Dad was offered another job, this time with a firm called I.J. Morgan in Taunton — I only remember that because Tessa and I made up a rhyme which went 'Silly old I.J. Morgan/Blows his nose like an organ', which must have annoyed our parents even more than the one about the banded krait in India.

We moved to an old rented farmhouse in a village not far from Taunton and went to the village school where all the classes were taught in the same room, and we developed Somerset accents. Tessa had a party piece: 'The cuckoo is a telltale, a mischief-making burrrrrrd, he floys to east, he floys to west, and whisperrrrrrs into every nest the wicked things he's hurrrrrrrrd.'

The folk in our village were like characters from *Cold Comfort Farm*: our cleaning lady, Ivy, and her husband were proud of the fact that they had not addressed a single word to each other for twenty years (messages were transmitted via their daughter, June), and we knew a grumpy farmer who never spoke to his family at all — at meals he would just stare fixedly at whatever he wanted passed to him, and eventually someone would notice and hand down the salt or salad cream or whatever it was. We could never imagine how he and his wife had ever managed to get together to produce children.

All my life I have been prone to sudden obsessions — in Fleet once, I doggedly modelled and painted little clay candleholders in the shape of choirboys (basically a cone shape with a round head on top). It was Prue's idea, and the local giftshop bought them from me at Christmas. In Somerset my craze was for curing mouse skins to sell to furriers. It had occurred to me that you never heard of coats made of mouse or rat, so there was obviously a gap in the market which I could fill and become rich. I found out about curing skins and bought alum from the chemist, and when all was ready I collected dead mice from the traps which were set around the farm and borrowed a sharp knife from the kitchen to cut and skin them with. But when I laid my first mouse corpse out on the chopping board, tummy up, and held my knife ready, I realised I could never cut it open and skin it, even if my life depended on it.

A more enduring passion was my collection of matchbox labels — why couldn't I have gone for something like Dinky Toys or Hornby trains that would now be worth a fortune? Matchbox labels are probably one of the very few items in the world that haven't gained an iota of value since the Fifties. I looked through one of my albums of labels recently and out fell a letter from the secretary of the British Governor of Uganda whom I had obviously plagued with correspondence. It is written on paper embossed with the words 'Government House', and is dated 15 January 1951; it reads, 'Dear Brigid. Both your letters, the one you wrote in November, and the second one written on 6 January, reached His Excellency the Governor; but I am afraid that whoever told you that he collected matchbox tops made a mistake for he does not do so. All I can do is return your own tops and hope that you may be able to find someone else to 'swap' with.'

Mum and Dad gave me four hens for my birthday that year — I think it was to teach me responsibility or perhaps to make up for the failure of my mouse-coat enterprise. I was to look after them and collect their eggs and sell them to Mum to earn some pocket money. The hens were huge Rhode Island Reds and I was terrified of them, especially as they fought and pecked each other's feathers out so they had horrible bald patches as if someone had started plucking them for the oven. In the end I was too frightened to go into their enclosure so I used to throw their food over the netting and Mum had to collect the eggs. Eventually she took them over altogether.

★ ★ ★

Two or three classes above me at the village school (meaning she was about fourteen), there was a farmer's daughter called Marge who was having an affair with a boy called Eddie, a young cowman (I've changed the names). She wondered if I'd like to watch them 'doing it' at their next rendezvous in a barn. I said yes — I was genuinely curious, but Eddie said no.

It was all very simple and innocent in those days — somehow even Marge and Eddie seemed quite innocent. Tessa and I thought the naughtiest thing we'd ever heard was my mother's story about some boys she'd known when she was young who would look in the phone book for people called Smelly and then ring them up and ask, 'Are you Smelly?' and when they said yes, the boys would say, 'Well, what are you going to do about it? Ha ha ha.'

But gradually the bad old outside world was beginning to impinge — I think my parents took

the *Daily Sketch* as well as *The Times* because I
was horrified by the sensational stories in some
tabloid at home and it couldn't have been the
*Mail* because that was a broadsheet in those
days, and it wouldn't have been the *Daily Mirror*
because that was LABOUR. (My grandmother
would never buy TUC biscuits because she
believed they were made by the Trades Union
Congress.)

The first news story that shocked me was the
appalling murder of the Drummond family in
1952: Sir Jack Drummond, a distinguished
biochemist, was camping in the South of France
along with his wife and daughter and they were
all killed one night, for apparently no reason.
(The murder was never solved satisfactorily.) Oh
God, I remember thinking, no one is safe
anywhere. That same year another violent case
made banner headlines — a shoot-out on the
roof of a warehouse in London between the
police and two young men, Christopher Craig
and Derek Bentley. A policeman was killed and
Bentley was hanged the following year. There
was huge discussion about this across the nation
— and at home — because he had not been the
one to pull the trigger, but he was older (twenty)
and had shouted 'Let him have it' to the younger
man (sixteen) with the gun.

But there were heroes as well as villains:
Captain Carlsen who clung for days to his
stricken ship, the *Flying Enterprise*, until just
minutes before it sank off Falmouth (the exact
opposite of the Italian captain who, fifty years
later, became famous for abandoning the *Costa*

*Concordia* and its passengers). And there were newspaper celebs too — I remember everyone at home tut-tutting over Lady Docker who, in the early Fifties, was the first person I can think of who was famous for no other reason apart from the fact that she was married to a very rich man and had a golden Daimler car.

★   ★   ★

After a while, Tessa and I were packed off from the farmhouse to what had once been a large convent near Taunton, but now had only a couple of dozen or so boarders. I hated not being at home with our parents, especially as they lived in the same county and I couldn't really understand why we'd been sent away. Only the other day my brother-in-law suggested that it was probably because our mother wanted to play bridge, and perhaps that was it, but it could have just been because putting your children in boarding school then was the 'done thing'. Whatever the reason we were there, I cried all the time — the nuns said I was washing all the colour out of my eyes — but I think Tessa must have quite liked it because I remember having to urge her to cry too, so that they would send us home, but of course they didn't.

In my homesickness I wet my bed, which brought the punishment of having to sleep alone in a dormitory that had twenty empty beds in it, which of course made me wet the bed even more. But back in my proper dorm it wasn't much better; the other girls used to throw my beloved teddy bear, Valena, a distinguished 'older woman' in my eyes (she had been my sister Moira's), from one side of the room to the other, and because she was ancient and bald they said she didn't look like a bear but a pig, and since she had no eyes and was shabby, they said she probably had fleas and named her Flea Pig. I felt such hurt and humiliation on behalf of my old friend — I imagine it felt a bit like being a mother whose child is being bullied. After the holidays, I never again took her out in public, but kept her in my bedroom at home which I shared with Tessa.

Tessa and I still bickered and argued non-stop and this led to the worst punishment we ever had. It happened one half-term at home: Dad warned that if we didn't stop quarrelling he would take us back to school for the rest of the holiday — and we didn't, and he did. Crying and pleading, clinging to the banisters, on to the front door — nothing melted his heart: we were told to get into the car and were driven back to school. Following that trauma, we managed to live peacefully together by dividing our room with a piece of string that neither of us was allowed to cross; later we were given separate rooms (I loved mine passionately and painted all the terrible brown junkshop-type furniture pale turquoise-blue).

\* \* \*

My moment of glory at the convent — rapidly followed by total humiliation — came when I was chosen to play the part of God the Father in the school concert. I had to stand on a table hidden behind a tall screen so as to be mysterious, and recite the gospel of St John: 'In the beginning was the Word . . . ' I was doing fine until the screen fell down and God the Father was revealed in school uniform perched on a table, and the parents in the audience started to giggle. In the end even I could see that it was funny. My real acting triumph came on another occasion when, sadly, there were no parents present, just nuns and girls. I was squashed into a cardboard box with a TV-screen-shaped hole cut in it so that only my face showed, and acted the part of the hugely popular TV presenter Sylvia Peters. No one remembers her now, but she was on the original *Come Dancing* and was the person chosen to present the Coronation in 1953; she also trained the Queen for her Christmas speeches — which is probably why, if you listen to the Queen's voice and Sylvia Peters's voice, they are indistinguishable one from another.

One of the younger nuns at school was a brilliant storyteller — but to this day I have never been able to be in a room at night without the curtains drawn because of her tale of someone seeing the devil's face pressed against a window in the dark. That was frightening enough, but then army friends of my parents rented a house that turned out to be seriously haunted and wrote an account — it was a diary — of their life there. We were not even supposed to know they'd *had* any such experience, let alone read the diary, but of course we children overheard them talking about it and 'borrowed' the diary from Mum's room and ever since then the combination of their terrifying ghost stories, plus the nun's tales, plus *Daily Sketch* crime stories, plus the scary memories from India, has meant that I cannot stay alone anywhere that isn't on a second or third floor with four locks on the doors and windows for fear of ghosts/ burglars/murderers. (Years later, when I became a journalist, I tried to persuade my parents' friends to publish their extraordinary diary, but by then their children had grown up and had careers and they didn't want the kind of publicity this would bring — but I often remember it and still think it would make a gripping book, and it must still be around somewhere . . . )

\* \* \*

My best pal at school was called Fatty (I was known as Beaky because my initials were BK). Fatty and I drew up a written pledge vowing that we would never wear lipstick, and signed it in our BLOOD. I think this was because we'd decided we hated grown-ups, especially our mothers (who wore lipstick), because they had sent us away to school in the first place. At that time I must have looked an even worse sight than I'd been in the days when my mother and aunt thought I was so plain, because by now I had a plate to straighten my teeth, as well as glasses — which I got by pretending I couldn't read the eye test, I so badly wanted them as I felt they were glamorous.

Aside from having ordinary friends like Fatty, all the younger girls at school seemed to have passionate crushes on the older ones. I'd never come across this before, but soon developed my own which was on the sporty games captain, Grania Fetherstonhaugh (I have not made this name up), whom I worshipped from a distance. As far as I know, everyone's passions remained this way — from a distance; the nearest we got to our heroines was to send them holy pictures with doting messages on the back. Just before I left this school at around twelve years old, I received my own admiring holy picture from one of the new girls. She was called Vivien, I couldn't really believe it, and to this day wonder if someone was pulling my leg or felt sorry for me.

★   ★   ★

Tessa and I had to leave the convent when my father got a job in Aldershot and we moved back to my grandparents' house in Fleet. By now they had died, and the house had been converted into two flats — we Keenans had the top one, and my widowed Aunt Thea and Jinny and Prue and Simon lived downstairs. We pushed a Hoover tube through the floor in the corner of our dining room and this became our homemade house phone for family communications. I was sent as a day girl to Farnborough Convent and Dad ferried me to Fleet station to catch the train every morning — we were nearly always late because I was never ready in time, and that quite often meant having to run down the platform and make a terrifying leap on to the moving train, something that still comes into my dreams.

The Coronation of Queen Elizabeth was looming; somehow Dad got two tickets for it and promised me I could go with him if I gave up biting my nails. I had always bitten my nails — despite bitter aloes painted on them, a special plate with loops over my teeth so they couldn't meet to bite, plasters on my fingers, gloves on my hands; all backed up with hundreds of firm resolutions, but I could not give up the habit. A place at the Coronation was the ultimate bribe and I really *meant* to stop, but when the Great Nail Inspection came, I failed it — Dad took Moira instead. Miserable, I decided to run away and packed a little cardboard attaché case. Halfway down the road I met Aunt Thea. 'Where are you off to?' she asked. 'I am running away,' I said sulkily. 'Oh,' she said, 'that's a pity, we are having scones for tea.' Greed overcame rage and self-hatred and I turned back. (I went on biting my nails for decades; definitely not a good look — especially for a fashion editor, as I was later to become. I held cigarettes and wine glasses with my knuckles, or wore Eylure false nails that risked coming off at any moment, and then — just as built-on artificial nails were invented which would have solved my problem — I gave up the habit, surprisingly in Kazakhstan which, of all AW's postings, is the one that gave me the greatest stress.)

In the meantime the rest of us watched the

Coronation on television at our neighbours' house. They were a mother and daughter: the mother was ancient and had an eye that looked, rather disgustingly, as if it was popping out; the daughter, also old, was strict but kind. They were the only people we knew who owned a television — it had a small screen with a kind of magnifying glass over it, and wasn't anything like the ones we watch today, but they were generous with it, cramming chairs into their sitting room for all the important 'national' occasions: the Coronation, the Boat Race, the Grand National and any big sporting events. These all seemed to be about running, with the four-minute-mile record being broken every week in the Fifties, but what strikes me now is how *white* British sports were then — all the athletic stars were thin, sinewy, white men with hairy legs like Roger Bannister and Chris Chataway.

Everyone in Britain looked at the same TV programmes in those days because there wasn't any choice; as soon as there were more channels available this didn't happen again for decades — until quite recently with the coming of brilliant series such as *The Wire* or *The Killing* or *Spiral* or *Wolf Hall* — not to mention *MasterChef* — which have reunited the viewing public again.

In the early Fifties everyone seemed to read the same books as well (I still have some of them: *The Kon-Tiki Expedition*, *Seven Years in Tibet* and *The Ascent of Everest*, passed down from my parents), and we watched the same films, mostly war movies then — *The Wooden*

*Horse, Above Us the Waves, The Colditz Story, The Cruel Sea* (from the book which was notorious among teenagers because it had rude bits in it) — so that as far as we children were concerned the war had been won by the actors Jack Hawkins, Richard Todd, John Mills, Michael Redgrave and John Gregson. My own favourite film was *Where No Vultures Fly*, about a game warden in Africa, with Anthony Steel and Dinah Sheridan (in Horrockses frocks). It was the big 'family' film of 1951; every person now my age was probably taken to see it as a child. I *loved* it — because of its African location which felt a bit like India to me — much more than I did *Genevieve*, the next great blockbuster starring Kay Kendall and Kenneth More, which came out two years later.

★  ★  ★

Our cousins were all away at school by now, and it wasn't long before Tessa and I were both sent off to board at Farnborough Convent, but during the holidays, especially when Moira came down from London at the weekends to join us, it was like being in an Enid Blyton sort of family of six, aged between nine and nineteen. (David was married by now and had left home.) The others used to tease me about having a big mouth, and once betted me that I would not be able to fit a whole orange into it. Triumphantly, I manoeuvred the orange in — but it lodged behind my front teeth and blocked up my nose and my throat so that I couldn't breathe, and they were all so busy laughing that they didn't notice I was suffocating. I was grunting and waving my arms in panic when Moira suddenly realised what was happening — but there was absolutely no way to pull out the orange, so she cut a hole in the bit that showed at the front of my wide-open mouth, and then squeezed my cheeks to get the juice out until the orange was shrunken enough to remove, and I survived.

Dad's land-agency duties in Aldershot involved the disused Longmoor Military Railway which most people weren't even aware existed — and that is how he knew that the Hollywood superstars Ava Gardner and Stewart Granger were coming there to film *Bhowani Junction*, a story by John Masters about Indian freedom fighters trying to blow up a train. Ava Gardner played an Anglo-Indian woman and Stewart Granger a British officer (in love with her of course). Dad arranged for us to go and watch the filming which was extra thrilling as it had to be done at night in the dark. Tessa did — probably still does — a good imitation of me tripping along the railway line in my little Louis heels (I'd dressed up) holding out my autograph book and calling: 'Miss Gardner, Miss Gardner . . . '

★   ★   ★

At the convent one of our schoolmates was Anne Robinson (later known for *The Weakest Link* on TV). I read somewhere that she hated the place, but I quite liked it: most of the nuns were Irish

106

(as usual) and superstitious, and would say things like 'There goes Brigid Keenan doing the Devil's work on earth' or 'Look at Tessa Keenan being blown along by the Devil like a little piece of fluff' — and though I was hopeless at Latin and maths, and spent many miserable hours shivering on the muddy hockey/lacrosse pitch, we had a good English teacher and there were lots of other girls who lived abroad and had seen the world outside Hampshire, as we had done. (When she came back from India, my poor sister Moira got into trouble at her school because every time the geography teacher mentioned a place — Delhi, Lahore, Basra, Damascus, Beirut, Marseilles or Paris — she'd put up her hand and say, 'I've been there,' which of course she had, but the teacher accused her of lying.) My own lasting friend from that time, Diana, who lived in Guyana, came to school in England on a banana boat from Trinidad.

The most shameful thing I did at Farnborough Convent was in my early days there: my form-mates and I put a waste-paper basket on top of the door so it would fall on our biology (bilge) teacher. All went according to plan except the teacher burst into tears and we were all appalled and mortified to have caused such distress. I still regret my part in it.

The star event of my schooldays — because it felt just like something out of an old-fashioned boarding-school story — was the midnight feast we held in my last term. We boarders couldn't leave the school grounds, but day-girls were commissioned to buy us various things to eat and drink, and we all sneaked out of our rooms and met, at midnight, under the stage, and tucked into the food we'd brought — all the time trembling with a kind of delicious fear that we would be discovered. Amazingly we weren't.

The organisers of the midnight feast included two of my best friends, Brenda Tandy (niece of the actress, Jessica Tandy) and Ann Coxon; we have stayed in touch. Ann Coxon became a high-powered doctor in Harley Street and, surprisingly perhaps, for the ex-head-girl of a convent, converted to Islam. Brenda met a rich Italian textile magnate not long after leaving school and it looked as though her story would have a fairytale ending, but at a society wedding in Turin, she leaned against a first-floor balcony for the photographer, and it gave way — she fell on to steps below, breaking her back. At the time, her husband made all the exquisite, pale, double-faced gaberdine fabrics for the popular couturier Courrèges, but then, suddenly, almost overnight it seemed, Yves Saint Laurent became everyone's favourite Paris designer with his garments in black or navy jersey, and the textile firm, not equipped to make knitted cloth, went bust, and shortly after this catastrophe Brenda's husband died. She has spent the rest of her life in a wheelchair, has raised three children with no one to support her, and no income apart from what she earned herself in a career as a fashion consultant. She has had the most difficult path, but all through it she has never ceased to be glamorous and indomitable, and I admire her more than anyone on earth. I sometimes think back to that midnight feast when, of course, none of us had any idea of what the future held.

\* \* \*

At Landour in the holidays we occasionally put on plays for the adults. Prue wrote these and sent us the scripts to learn at school, so we'd be ready to start rehearsing as soon as we got home. Once I had to play Dr Watson in a Sherlock Holmes-type drama; my lines, in verse, included the words 'pursued by robber bands', but when I spoke them they came out as 'pursued by *rubber* bands' and the play came to a sudden end with the cast collapsed in a heap of giggles. The passion for dressing up started again — it went on for years in various forms. Aunt Joan (who by now had become an air hostess working with a long-forgotten airline called Airwork at Black-bushe airport near Camberley) got engaged to a short, bald man whom we nicknamed the Golf Ball. One evening while she was waiting nervously for him to collect her for a date, we thought it would be funny for one of us (I think Prue was chosen) to dress up in a man's suit, put a pudding basin on her head and kneel in the hall on a pair of men's shoes, pretending to be the Golf Ball, to tease Joan. Of course he arrived early and Prue's act had to be explained away — but I don't suppose it crossed his mind that a teenage girl kneeling on the floor with a pudding basin on her head was supposed to be him.

Or perhaps it did, because the relationship didn't last and Aunt Joan then became engaged to a dashing Dutchman. Her future mother-in-law, who was wealthy and smart and lived in Mayfair (which impressed us all because of Monopoly), invited her to treat herself to some new underwear at Harrods as a present. Joan went and bought some pretty things, as well as a new roll-on (a roll-on was a sort of elasticated corset, a bit like Spanx knickers without the crotch), and then, not wanting to take her own disgusting, old grey and perished roll-on away with her, she hid it behind the radiator in the changing room. To her horror, Harrods found it, and sent it to her mother-in-law-to-be who asked if it was hers. She denied all knowledge of it, and she married the Dutchman.

Around this time — I had just started commuting every day to secretarial school in London — a young American called Charlie Hudson, a friend of cousins in Philadelphia, wrote to our mother to say he was touring England and could he come and stay with us? AN AMERICAN! FROM AMERICA, THE PROMISED LAND! COMING TO STAY! I immediately developed a crush on him although I had never set eyes on him.

To tease me, the family created a brilliant life-size dummy, 'Charlie Hudson', and one day propped him up on the sofa in my parents' sitting room upstairs. When Dad fetched me off the train from London he said, 'We must get back quickly, Charlie's arrived . . . ' I was thrilled and quickly touched up my lipstick and powdered my nose in the car, and rushed up the outside stairs to our flat to meet the famous

American. Everyone was gathered there ready to join in the joke when I discovered that 'Charlie' was a dummy, and we were all shrieking with laughter when THE REAL CHARLIE HUDSON arrived, earlier than expected, at our upstairs front door. Panic ensued, we couldn't explain away the dummy on the sofa, so my mother picked it up and threw it out of the window. But then there was a new problem: how to stop Charlie Hudson going anywhere near the window and seeing a corpse lying on the lawn below. 'Oh my! What a beautiful English garden you have,' he said, approaching the window eagerly; he had to be tugged back, literally, by my father.

Another dressing-up joke nearly ended in death. One afternoon we children put a ladder up to the same sitting-room window and opened it, so that later in the evening, Simon, disguised as a burglar, with some of his teeth blackened out, could climb up and appear through the curtains while we were all watching telly (we had just got our own by this time). It had been carefully planned so we cousins knew this was going to happen, but no one had foreseen our father's reaction — he vaulted over the sofa and grabbed Simon by the neck, shouting, 'I've got you, you bastard,' and tried to push him back off the ladder. Simon was shrieking, 'UNCLE JOHN! IT'S ME, SIMON!', but Dad was too full of adrenalin to understand, and we had to pull him off poor Simon.

Looking back at those years, it seems we had so much fun despite not having a computer or iPads or Kindles or mobiles or games consoles — we were so easily pleased. On Sundays, when all the shops were firmly closed, the family would happily go for a drive — sometimes to look at something specific, but more often than not just ambling about in the car looking at the scenery. (Our grandparents had done this too, in their Morris with its huge mudguards and running-boards — its number was BOR 718, and it's a puzzle to me why I can remember that, when I can't always remember the numberplate of my own car now.)

Occasionally there would be a TREAT — a coach trip from Fleet to something cultural in London. Going to London was an event that involved dressing up: Mum would wear a hat — women never went out without hats or headscarves and gloves in those days — and Dad would wear a bowler. *Every* man wore a bowler — Waterloo Bridge at commuter times was a sea of bobbing black bowlers, and then at some point — in the late Seventies? In the early Eighties? — they vanished as suddenly and completely as the Indian vulture.

We were usually taken to matinees — at the Old Vic for Shakespeare, Covent Garden for the ballet and to 'suitable' musicals: I still find myself singing bits of the songs from *The Boy Friend* and *Salad Days*, and I can recite that first verse of 'The Hippopotamus Song' ('Mud, mud, glorious mud'), from *At the Drop of a Hat* with Flanders and Swann that has gone into the British DNA.

Outside Harrods, on one of the London trips,

Mum and Dad bumped into Danny Kaye whose films (*Hans Christian Andersen, The Court Jester, Knock on Wood*) we'd seen and adored. They knew his face so well, but could not remember his name, so after they had exchanged smiles, Mum said, 'I'm so sorry, I know we've met at the Bridge Club in Fleet, but I can't remember your name,' and he said, 'Danny Kaye,' and they were overwhelmed with embarrassment.

My twelfth birthday treat was an outing to *The Mousetrap* and I screamed so loudly Dad said I would have to go out if I did it again. And during the Festival of Britain we were taken to the Pleasure Gardens in Battersea Park where we went on the Rotor which was the biggest thrill of all time. (To ride the Rotor you went into a giant metal drum, stood with your back against the wall, and then the whole thing spun round so fast that when they lowered the floor — and everyone screeched with fear — you remained glued to the wall by centrifugal force.)

There were lots of young people the same ages as us in Fleet, mostly children of other army, or service, families, and we entertained ourselves pottering about locally on our bikes, or going for walks or playing tennis. Occasionally we'd make an excursion to the Lido swimming pool in Aldershot or to the cinema there where movies were seen through a fog of cigarette smoke and part of the entertainment was the witty barracking from the soldier audience. Once, on a cinema outing with my parents, a soldier dropped a huge lump of something sticky

— bubble gum or toffee — between me and my seat back. It hardened over the hours I unknowingly leaned on it, and glued me to the seat so firmly that I had to struggle to stand up for the National Anthem at the end of the evening under Dad's stern eye.

Everything then seemed wonderful — or is it just that looking back from a distance of over sixty years has coloured it all with a rose tint? In my memory now, Hawley Lake, where we often went, lots of us together, to swim (and, in my case, to show off my new pink 'playsuit'), is as glamorous as the French Riviera. I don't ever want to go back there and discover that it is really just a pool of black murky water surrounded by mud.

★  ★  ★

How anyone went on holidays abroad in the Fifties and Sixties baffles me as British currency restrictions meant that for much of the time you could only take forty-five pounds to spend. How we as a family ever went abroad baffles me even more, because my parents never had any money, but they were extremely thrifty, they saved, and somehow managed to give us great adventures: we went on pilgrimages by coach to Lourdes and to the Passion Play at Oberammergau, we had skiing holidays twice (more coach trips), and a couple of times we stayed with friends in Majorca where I went through the falling-in-love-with-a-Spanish-waiter/ Ernest-Hemingway/bullfighting/*The-Sun-Also-Rises*/

114

adolescent-English-girl-in-Spain ritual (we did actually see the great El Cordobés fight in Majorca on one of these holidays). Or we would go in our old car to the South of France and stay in a cheap hotel or with other friends there. At first, wherever we were Dad spoke Hindustani, but after a while he developed a vocabulary of simple French and Spanish words mixed together, e.g., *merçias*. In France once he asked for directions at a crossroads — '*Ici* or *aussi*,' he said, indicating the two roads. '*Aussi*,' pointed the Frenchman without batting an eye. At the tourist information office in Palma once (booking the El Cordobés bullfight tickets actually) he was trying to find the woman with white hair who had been so helpful earlier in the morning, so he asked, '*Donde esta la madame avec les chevaux blanco?*', which could be translated as 'Where is the lady with the white horses?', but they understood him immediately.

Dad was not a good driver — in the early days of motorways and motorway cafés in France, we watched from our table as he reversed into an empty police car parked outside (embarrassingly, the *gendarmes* from the car were sitting next to us and watching him too, whooping and cheering him on). He once won some sort of award from the British police for careful driving; they said it was because he had indicated 'well in advance' that he was going to turn right, but we all secretly thought that he'd probably had the indicator out all morning. On the other hand, there were very few motorways and no satnavs in those days, and it amazes me now that Dad

115

managed to get us right across France — including through French cities like Rouen and Lyons — quite regularly, as well as finding our way in Spain, even to the door of our hotel in some back street in Barcelona, so I shouldn't criticise his driving.

It was in France that my new best friend Anne and I heard that an American aircraft carrier, the *Newport News*, had docked in Villefranche-sur-Mer not far from where we were staying. We must have been fifteen then, on holiday with our parents and our younger siblings, Tessa and Anne's brother Simon, and slightly bored, and thought it would be nice to meet some sailors. When everyone believed we were asleep we got dressed, put on lipstick, crept out and started walking to Villefranche. Luckily for us, Simon and Tessa, who were obviously slightly more sensible than we were, decided to alert the parents. Anne and I were collected off the dark road to Villefranche by two furious fathers — I still breathe a sigh of relief when I think of it.

Some of our holidays took us home to our roots in Ireland. We once went to a place called Glendalough in County Wicklow where I scrambled up to the top of a grassy bank, straightened up under a wooden sign to St Kevin's Kitchen which I hadn't noticed and was knocked out cold — my body must have dropped like a stone because it squashed a mouse that I fell on. (They found it when they picked me up.) I came round in the car, hearing Dad, who was normally famous for his charm, being brusque with someone who'd offered to help. 'Not unless you are a qualified doctor,' Dad was saying, but I suppose he was anxious.

I didn't seem to have much luck in Ireland — in the chaos of our arrival on an earlier family visit to meet our great-grandmother in Dublin, my finger got slammed in the car door. Just as I was getting over that trauma I was told to take my chewing gum out of my mouth and come and say hello, politely, to Great-Granny. Stupidly I stuck the chewing gum in the palm of my hand which she then shook (I thought she would kiss me) and when my hand came back the gum had gone.

Before beginning the journey home to England by ferry after one of these Irish trips, Mum and Aunt Thea spent some time winding cloth around their top halves, over their bras, under their jumpers, and shrieking with laughter — much to the bafflement of us children. They didn't really explain what they were doing, but I think that fabric must have been rationed in England and not in Ireland, and so, being keen dressmakers (almost everyone made their own clothes in those days), they were smuggling some home.

Twice, along with our cousins and Aunt Thea, we went to stay in a convent in Brittany which took paying guests. We loved these particular holidays because all the family was together, the beaches were vast and there were activities on them organised by something called the As-Mickey Club — where we met other children we could hate together; plus the local café had a *baby-foot* machine (table football), and we were

117

free to roam around. The convent locked its doors early in the evening and we liked the fact that if the grown-ups had been out having drinks they had to climb through our bedroom windows to get in again.

I blame one of these holidays for turning me into the most indecisive person in the world. Dad took Tessa and me to a souvenir shop and told us to pick one little thing each as a present. Tessa chose quickly, but I hummed and hawed and couldn't make up my mind between a small china clog and a tiny painted plate. This went on for so long that Dad began to get irritated, and then the shop owner said, 'Ah, let the leetle girl 'ave both, and I will only charge you for one zing.' That was it — since then I have never been able to make a decision about anything, probably because my subconscious is telling me that if I drag it out long enough I can have it all.

★   ★   ★

In 1956 the Hungarian Revolution took place. You wouldn't think this could possibly have any bearing on our lives in Fleet, but in fact a big camp was set up for the refugees in the nearby barracks in Crookham, and we all volunteered to go and help; my job involved helping to sort the hundreds of donated men's shirts into sizes. (In all, 22,000 Hungarian refugees came to Britain; not all of them were in the camp near Fleet, of course, but they got a good reception wherever they went — unlike the welcome their country has given to the recent influx of refugees from

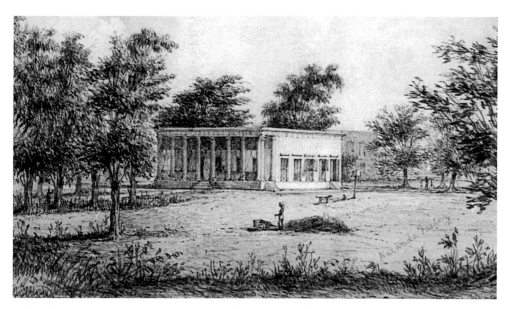

My French great-great-grandfather's silk factory, Nakanda,
in Bengal. The drawing was done by his son, Albert Dubus,
in 1862. Quite recently AW and I went to India on a mission to
try and find this place – we failed, but are still on the case.

My mother, left, and her sister Dorothy (Aunt Thea) – both
looking distinctly apprehensive – with Jacko, their father's pet
gibbon; my grandmother and the ayah are behind. The picture
was taken in their garden in Madras (Chennai).

At the caves of Ellora and Ajanta in India, 1948, with Dad and Swaller (sitting bolt upright). Tessa and I are looking quiet as we have just had a major ticking-off for fighting.

In St-Yrieix-la-Perche during my French exchange in the summer of 1956. My best friend Anne (also doing an exchange) is on the far left; the French friends we were staying with are on the right.

Paris, 1957. I took this picture of my fellow students at Mademoiselle Anita's finishing school on an afternoon outing with Mademoiselle Marguerite, our guide and chaperone. We are all about seventeen but look more like thirty.

The modest home of my French schoolfriend Daisy de Montesson, who invited me to stay during the Suez Crisis; no wonder I was a tiny bit daunted.

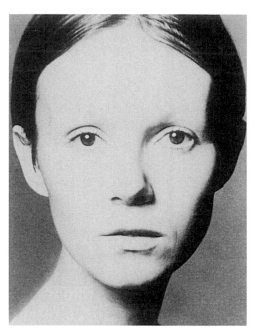
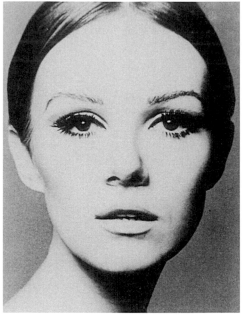

© *Peter Knapp*

Nicole de Lamargé was one of the greatest models – she could adapt her look to suit any outfit. These 'before and after' pictures of her with and without make-up were taken in 1966 for the hugely influential *Elle* magazine by Peter Knapp, the photographer and art director who was her partner at the time.

This picture of the Beatles' women was taken by Ronald Traeger for my farewell fashion article for the *Sunday Times*, in the autumn of 1967, before I went off to try and be a war correspondent. From left: Pattie Harrison, Cynthia Lennon and Maureen Starr; in front is Pattie's sister, Jenny. They are all wearing hippy clothes by a group of Dutch designers who called themselves The Fool.

© *Ronald Traeger*

My Jane Fonda moment – and possibly my most embarrassing picture ever: posing with a mortar shell at the Filipino base in Tây Ninh, Vietnam. I honestly only did it to please our hosts.

The photographer Norman Eales could make anyone look glamorous: he took this picture of me for a *Sunday Times* feature in which the women's-page writers chose what we wanted for Christmas. The article was mostly done to please advertisers and I *had* to choose this coat because it came from one of them – which is not to say I wouldn't have liked it.

the Middle East.) Lots of the refugees seemed to be performers of one kind or another. A friend of ours who was helping list their qualifications for jobs in Britain asked a man who'd said he was a lion tamer if he could do anything else, and he said, 'Oh yes, I can tame tigers too.' Aunt Thea made lifelong friends with a charming couple who were illusionists.

I only worked in the camp for about a week in the Christmas holidays, but naturally I developed a crush on a young, gypsy-looking Hungarian — I don't remember his name now. We hardly spoke because we had no common language, but exchanged addresses and wrote to each other a couple of times: he from Canada where he had been sent to make a new life, and me from Paris where I was at finishing school. My local church, Saint Pierre de Chaillot, had a Hungarian priest who used to translate the letters — quite sadly for me, there was never anything in them that couldn't be shown to the Father.

*   *   *

Eventually all of us young left home to go to work or train in London or elsewhere, and Landour, the big Edwardian house in Fleet, was sold (for a pittance — no one realised it was going to be pulled down and half a dozen houses built in its place). Dad took a break from land agency because he was offered a job running a Catholic club in London. This was entirely staffed by Irish people, with a shifty-looking barman who ruled the roost. Tessa lived there with Mum and Dad, and I used to leave the flat I shared with Moira and go and stay when I felt homesick for the family.

One morning in the dining room we placed our breakfast order with Brigid, the waitress; nothing happened for a very long time and then Brigid's sister, who also worked there, came and said she was sorry everything was running late but Brigid had just had a baby upstairs (she hadn't known she was pregnant). It was all very Irish and very Catholic — it could have been scripted by Edna O'Brien — and there were endless problems, but the last straw was when Dad found out that the barman had tried to tunnel through the wall of the gents' cloakroom into the back of the safe in the office. It was discovered because, Irishly, he missed his mark and came out in the middle of the wall. Dad eventually returned to his old land-agent job with relief, and Mum and Dad went back to live near Fleet, where we would join them at weekends.

It seems to me now that my childhood was the exact opposite of a misery memoir — apart from the time spent at boarding school, it was almost *too* happy, too sheltered, too cosy. Is that possible? It took me years to gain any confidence outside my family circle: we had so much fun together that I never really wanted to separate myself from them or grow up at all. In fact, I still haven't quite got used to the idea.

# 5

Though I say it myself, I was a bit of a star in the Sixties — actually, to be strictly accurate, I was not a star, but a meteor. And as a matter of fact I don't have to say it myself because I was officially designated as one in a book written by Jonathan Aitken, best known now as the Tory MP who went to prison for telling a lie on oath, but back then celebrated as the author of *The Young Meteors*, the bible on the Sixties. I found a copy of the book in a charity shop the other day and looked myself up — I was twenty-seven at the time it was written, working on the *Sunday Times*, and Jonathan Aitken describes me as being *one of the two best young fashion writers of the day*. (The other one was Georgina Howell, then at the *Observer*, who, like me, left the fashion world long ago and now writes books, including a great biography of Gertrude Bell.)

J.A. quotes me as saying: 'Certainly we fashion editors have a lot of power, but I like to think we use it discriminately.' I can't imagine ever saying anything like that in a million years — and as for 'discrimination', that has never really been my strong suit.

When Jonathan Aitken asked to interview me for the book, I invited him to dinner and then panicked as I couldn't think what to cook for him, or who to ask with him. In the end I decided on a pork fillet stuffed with prunes (I like to think that the recipe came from Robert Carrier's *Great Dishes of the World* which was THE best-selling cookbook at the time, but I can't really remember), and I had a trial run, inviting my sister Tessa and Malcolm, her boyfriend (later, husband), and when I served the cooked fillet they took one look at it and said, 'Oh God, you'll have to cut it up or do something with it because it looks exactly like a horse's willy on the dish.'

★   ★   ★

My glittering career as a young meteor was all a mistake really — in fact it was the last thing I ever intended, because a friend of my mother's from the Bridge Club in Fleet once said to me, 'You don't want to be a career girl, my dear, men never like that at all.' My future had been mapped out by my parents — basically in accordance with what middle-class people like us did then — and I went along with it since I didn't know anything, and hadn't any better ideas. Their plan set out that I would leave Farnborough Convent after GCEs, go to a smart finishing school, be presented at Court, and then do a secretarial course after which I would work as a secretary for a couple of years until I got married. (University, even A levels, didn't come into it much for girls in the Fifties.) That was supposed to be how it went, but somehow, after the first part, it didn't quite work out like that.

The finishing school was in Paris, it was called Mademoiselle Anita's, and it just happened to be the smartest, most exclusive school on the planet at that time. How my mother found this place, and how she got them to take me as a student and how she paid for it, is a complete mystery that I have never managed to work out — especially the initial question: how on earth did she know about it?

It was not the first time I had been away in France — two years earlier I had done a French exchange with a girl, Marie-Ange, who came from a pleasant family whose nearest train station was Limoges. They met me there quite late in the evening and drove me to their home through silent villages of grey-shuttered houses that looked so un-English I immediately began to feel homesick.

My sister Moira had done an exchange too, several years before (how did my mother, in Fleet, find these French hosts? I wonder), and, because she was staying with grand-sounding people who lived in a château, Mum sent her off with homemade but smart clothes and party dresses — only to find that the family was penniless and more or less camping in their mansion which had been wrecked by the Germans in the war, and they were all wearing old trousers and jumpers and screamed with laughter at Moira when she unpacked her bag. For this reason I was dispatched with cotton slacks, only to discover that the father of 'my' family would not allow the women in his house to wear any kind of trousers, so I had to put on the same homemade red-and-white gingham skirt every day for three weeks.

I didn't get over my homesickness, though falling in love with Gilles, Marie-Ange's brother, helped a bit. I don't think he actually ever even noticed that I was there, but I read a lot of Georgette Heyer's romantic novels at that time, and lived in a completely unreal world in which it was entirely possible that a handsome, sophisticated 25-year-old Frenchman would see the hidden beauty in a dumpy fourteen-year-old in a skirt she'd made herself, and fall hopelessly in love with her.

★   ★   ★

The finishing school was the annexe to a convent — Le Couvent de l'Assomption — in the posh 16th arrondissement of Paris, and it was where the noblest and/or wealthiest families *in the world* sent their daughters to learn *savoir-faire* (how to behave) and *savoir-vivre* (how to live) — and how you must never trust a man with your little finger because if you do he will seize your whole body.

My schoolmates were princesses and countesses with names like Metternich and von Bismarck, Hohenlohe and Bourbon (the family of the kings of France before the Revolution), and I was very seriously out of my league. I was a boarder (which was even more exclusive and chic than being a day-girl) and there was only one other British boarder, Margaret. I was scared of her because, being a fellow-countrywoman, she knew that I had no business in this school, but then again, I knew that she didn't really either, and in the end we became friends.

Mademoiselle Anita was a terrifying person. Medium height and slightly stocky, with the most upright posture I have ever seen, she wore her grey hair scraped back into a perfect French pleat, was always dressed in black ankle-length gowns with old-fashioned but elegant laced-up shoes with heels, and carried a walking cane with a silver top. None of us girls ever knew her surname or anything else about her — was she the widow or the illegitimate daughter of a prince or a king, or could she be the victim of some aristocrat cad to whom she had entrusted her little finger?

We boarders were not allowed out with anyone who had not been personally interviewed by her, so you can imagine how many dates I had (i.e., none) except for one afternoon when, on the pretext of meeting another girl from school for a coffee, I managed to sneak off with a young Russian who was studying in Paris (though I'd met him at a party in England). I can't remember his name, which is strange, because Russians were an intriguing rarity in the West back then. He took me out for a ride on his motorbike — which means that I HAVE actually driven round Paris with my hair streaming in the warm wind, or whatever it was Marianne Faithfull sang that you had to do before you died. At the time, with no helmet, clinging to him from the back of the bike as it hurtled down the Champs Élysées, I just wished I was safely at school with my girlfriends. I never saw him again; Russians are not like us, I think he thought I was a bit wet.

All invitations had to be passed by Mademoiselle Anita as well, to make sure they were smart enough. I had very, very few and only one of them ever met with her enthusiasm — it was from a fellow pupil, a day-girl who was one of the daughters of Bao Dai, the last Emperor of Vietnam, exiled in Paris, asking me for lunch. At the meal a uniformed servant stood behind each of the many guests at the table, and when I wrote to my mother describing the amazing grandeur of it all, I didn't know what these men should be called — 'footmen' or 'butlers' didn't seem to be oriental or exotic enough — so I put innocently, 'There was a *eunuch* behind every chair.'

Some French friends of Mum's invited me to a wedding but I was not allowed to go because Mademoiselle Anita could see from the invitation or their names (I was never clear on this) that they were not quite 'the right kind of people'. I remember crying for the implied insult to my beloved mother.

Perhaps I should explain here how crucial 'class' was in those days — and not just in a smart finishing school in Paris, it was even more so in Britain itself. The words you used really mattered — your place in the social hierarchy was judged by them — and it was so cruel: a person could be cast into social outer darkness for saying 'pardon' or 'toilet' — terms which were deemed 'common'. Being 'common' was similar to, but worse, than being 'naff' or 'chav' now — an aristocrat can be 'naff' or 'chav' in their taste or behaviour, but they can't really be 'common' because that implies lowly birth. There were euphemisms for 'common' — 'not out of the top drawer', 'not one of us'. (And you had to be *extra* careful about being deemed 'not one of us' if you were an Irish-Catholic family from India, as we were, because those things in themselves were considered seriously dodgy — particularly if you were 'Indian educated', as my father was until he went to Sandhurst.)

My sisters and I were brought up to use all the right words: 'writing paper' never 'notepaper', 'scent' instead of 'perfume', 'sofa' instead of 'couch', 'coat and skirt' instead of 'suit', and so on. Even putting a letter into an envelope (*onvelope*, by the way) was fraught with class — you had to fold it so that the signature was on the *outside* of the paper, and you should never hold your knife like a pencil, put milk in before the tea, lick your fingers to turn newspaper pages, have pierced ears (Irish maids), wear jewellery during the day (pearls were OK), have a loo-paper holder in the bathroom (rolls of paper should be in a basket), wear white shoes or jumpers that were too tight, or whisper behind your hand as in the famous photograph of Hillary Clinton talking to Cherie Blair.

My cousin Simon went to Sandhurst to train as an army officer, and reported back that they were warned never ever to use the expression

'Give the cruet a fair wind, old chap', meaning pass the salt and pepper (cruet was a taboo word anyway), and on no account should they refer to an uncle as 'my avuncular relative'. (It was so bizarre to imagine anyone using either of those phrases that our family immediately took to saying them non-stop.)

As for our accents . . . I am amazed when I listen to old radio recordings to hear how clipped and grand middle-class people sounded in those days. They said *orf*, *plahstic*, *elahstic*, *sawft*, *frawst*, *Orstralia*, *Orstria*, *crawss*, and Catholics went to *Mahss*.

In 1956, the year I started at finishing school, Nancy Mitford edited a book, *Noblesse Oblige*; it was illustrated by the famous cartoonist of the day, Osbert Lancaster (little did I know that in years to come I would sit next to him in the office at the *Daily Express*), and included a satirical poem on how to get on in society by John Betjeman.

The book was a sort of jokey guide to improving your social status and Nancy Mitford listed all the words that were considered U (meaning upper class) and non-U (i.e., 'common') that we Keenan girls had been trained to use: *drawing room* was U, *lounge* non-U; *looking-glass* was U, *mirror* non-U; *children* was U, *kids* non-U; *pudding* was U, *sweet* non-U; *napkin* was U, *serviette* non-U; and so on. (In fact, the idea of U and non-U had actually been invented a couple of years before by a linguistics professor, Alan S.C. Ross, in an article about class in Britain for an academic journal in Finland, but Nancy

Mitford got all the credit.)

People rushed to buy *Noblesse Oblige* and the entire middle class of Britain became obsessed with U and non-U, and went round quoting Betjeman's poem at each other laughingly, to show how they themselves knew *perfectly* well what was what.

Phone for the fish knives, Norman,
As cook is a little unnerved;
You kiddies have crumpled the serviettes
And I must have things daintily served.
. . .
Now here is a fork for your pastries
And do use the couch for your feet;
I know that I wanted to ask you —
Is trifle sufficient for sweet?

To appreciate the in-jokes fully, there was a world of upper-class behaviour you had to know about apart from mere words, mainly that U people liked to keep things basic and restrained: no flashiness or glitz or showing off your money — even having central heating could be considered a bit 'nouveau-riche' back in the day (when, later, telephone answering machines were invented lots of U people wouldn't use them; indeed, some still don't) — and one should never ever try to be 'dainty' or 'refined' (U people never ate pastries with a fork or used fish knives or doilies, and so on). And 'cook' on its own wouldn't do; it should have been '*the* cook'.

Pronunciation was another whole can of worms — riding trousers were pronounced

129

*joedpurs* not jodhpurs, but then, the opposite, scones not *scoenes* . . . At home my aunt announced that she had it on good authority that laundry and hydrangea should be pronounced *lahndry* and *hydrahngea*, and that corgi was supposed to be *kergi*, but we didn't believe her.

In the final analysis, though, I think all this U and non-U hysteria helped to make the class system ridiculous, and hastened its end.

Just as I finished writing that paragraph, my eye fell on a quote in the *Guardian* from Lady Fellowes, wife of Julian Fellowes of *Downton Abbey* fame, in which she says that she and her husband often enjoy a quiet little laugh at guests who *fold their napkins* after a meal, or who tip their soup plate *towards* themselves, rather than away, so perhaps nothing has changed after all.

⋆　⋆　⋆

Back in Paris, one of our classes each week was midwifery — I hated this lesson (though I quite liked the bit about turning a drawer from a chest into an emergency baby's bed) and I made an appointment with Mademoiselle Anita to explain to her that I was never likely to have to deliver a baby and please could I be excused from the session.

'Absolutely not,' she snapped in French. 'You never know when someone on your estate might need your help.' I tried to point out that we lived in a flat in an Edwardian redbrick villa in Fleet — *Fleet* — and that the nearest thing to an estate in the lives of the Keenans would be a neighbouring council estate, but I could see that the very idea of Fleet was beyond her imagination, let alone our house in it; and I had to go back to the classes. So I know (or should I say knew, in case I am ever tested) how to deliver a baby, and how to bind the umbilical cord with thread (silk of course).

Far worse than the midwifery class, though, was our compulsory Social Service — one afternoon every week had to be given to good deeds; I was allocated to teach algebra in a home for girls who had been saved from prostitution. They were the same age or older than me and infinitely more worldly-wise and sophisticated — I was absolutely terrified of them: to this day when I see the name of the Métro station Gaîté written up, I start a panic attack. When I told the nuns that my algebra O-level mark was 8 out of 100, they changed my subject to English conversation; I remember the first time I timidly asked my class of about half a dozen girls if they could speak any English and they all laughed and one said, 'I can say keees me, Johnnie.' After that I read to them from English books while they dozed off.

When we went out and about in Paris, as we did most afternoons to see exhibitions and museums, our group of perhaps seven or eight teenage girls was escorted by a guide-cum-chaperone. Poor Mademoiselle Marguerite, she was a little old lady buttoned up in a navy overcoat and scarf, who we never saw without her squashed navy felt hat, and we tormented her by disappearing down alleyways, or hiding from her in the giant galleries of the Louvre, and then giving her a fright. But when I look at the group photographs of us students then, I can hardly believe that we were so mischievous because we seem like a bunch of middle-aged women.

Perhaps it was her revenge, but one day she took us to the military hospital at Val-de-Grâce, where we saw the most shocking wax masks of facial injuries from the two world wars: gaping holes where noses or eyes had been, lower jaws blown away and teeth exposed as on a skull — and these were from men who had *survived*. It took me years to erase the images of what I saw that day from my memory.

My particular pals at school were Blanca Guardiola, whose family bred the best fighting bulls in Spain; Tati from Mexico, whose mother died when she was small and no one told her about menstruation so for a long time she thought there was something wrong with her; Brigitte, my lovely Belgian roommate (who much later in life was briefly and unhappily in the headlines when she gave birth to septuplets who died); Mona from Lebanon, who was big and smoulderingly sexy; Marie-Sol, a lively Sicilian princess; and chic little Daisy de Montesson, who invited me to stay in her family's enormous château during the Suez Crisis when everyone else's parents took them home for fear of the upcoming global conflict (which didn't happen); mine couldn't afford to.

It was a bit of a nightmare at Daisy's as I didn't own an alarm clock and, no matter how earnestly I asked, no one woke me up in the mornings, so that every day I emerged, covered with confusion and embarrassment, just in time for lunch. Thinking about it now, it occurs to me that perhaps leaving me asleep was easier for them than having to entertain me.

\* \* \*

I don't know about the other pupils, but for me the most exciting school outing was when some elegant woman friend of Mademoiselle Anita's took us to the hushed grey and white showrooms of Christian Dior in the Avenue Montaigne where we saw his Spring 1957 collection — Dior himself was still alive then. It was a revelation: another world; I had never imagined in my wildest dreams that either clothes — or women — could be so beautiful. Later in life I was to see dozens of Paris collections, but nothing ever matched the wonder of that first one: I can still remember an exquisite white organdie dress embroidered with lilies-of-the-valley that I just wanted to stare at for ever.

When my younger sister Tessa followed me to Mademoiselle Anita's a couple of years later, as a day-girl, there was no outing to Dior, but there was a fashion show of sorts: the woman with whom Tessa and the other students lodged lived in the same building as the prime minister of France, Monsieur Debré, and she would take her girls into his apartment (she seemed to have a key) and they would look at the dresses in Madame Debré's wardrobe together. The

Debrés were living in the prime-ministerial residence, the Hôtel Matignon, so they were not there, but Tessa used to wonder nervously what on earth would happen if Madame came back unexpectedly and found all these girls examining her clothes . . .

*   *   *

Before leaving for school in Paris, I had developed a crush on a Fleet boy called Peter whom I had kissed once at a party. (At least this was a step up from having a passion for Gilles who hardly knew I was there, or for the brother of one of my convent schoolfriends whom I had only seen in a photograph.) I don't expect Peter had ever thought about me again, but I daydreamed about him all the time and one of the highlights of my stay in Paris was on Valentine's Day when I got a home-made card covered with cut-out lips of all sorts, with a message reading: 'I wish mine were on yours.' Of course I KNEW it was from Peter, and slept with it under my pillow — until the awful day a couple months later when I was leafing through the magazines in the school library and suddenly noticed that all the lips had been cut out of the pictures. My card was not from Peter but from my friends; how they must have laughed. (Actually they told me later that they hadn't, because I took it all so seriously that they feared for my mental health should I discover the truth.)

When I told this story to my daughter Claudia

not long ago, she said pityingly, 'Oh, Mum, as if any boy would *make* a card.'

★ ★ ★

Thinking about it now, I realise that my generation of girls in the Western world was/is perhaps the most fortunate in history: the Second World War was over, no other conflict had (as yet) engulfed the world, we were able to train and work and earn money, we had access to efficient birth control and we had independence. Our little group in Paris didn't understand most of that yet, but we had all been born in the years of the war and had known, to some degree (I was the luckiest), fear and instability, fathers away fighting (or taken prisoner or killed or wounded), food shortages, rationing, bombing raids — the French, Dutch and Belgian girls had lived through German occupation, and the persecution of the Jews — and we felt grateful, not only because we'd come out on the other side of all this, but because we now found ourselves in a kind of Promised Land. For it was not just the timing of our births in historical terms that was lucky, it was because a whole new world was being created especially for seventeen-year-olds like us as well. We were a new invention — TEENAGERS! Never before had our age group been looked on as particularly special, but now, it seemed, we were the most important people on earth. There was music being made especially for us — a far cry from the love stories of sad grown-ups like the jilted band leader and

135

poor Miss Otis of my brother's 78s; we had Frankie Laine with 'Cool Water', Tennessee Ernie Ford with 'Sixteen Tons', Paul Anka with 'Diana', Buddy Holly with 'Peggy Sue', Frank Sinatra with 'Come Fly with Me', Pat Boone and so many others, but it was really Bill Haley's 'Rock Around the Clock', which hit the charts in 1955, that changed everything. I remember the first time I heard it — before the nuns at my convent banned it as 'animal music' — getting gooseflesh all over. I still do. And the music was all the more extraordinary when you think that Bill Haley was middle-aged, with a terrible kiss-curl on his forehead, and one of his musicians (the Comets, they were called) was actually born in VICTORIAN times. But then again, among our romantic heroes then was the singer Johnnie Ray, who wore a *hearing aid* and still sold more than two million copies of 'Cry'.

And then, in 1956, there was the volcanic eruption of Elvis with 'Heartbreak Hotel'. What can I say? We girls in Paris — like teenagers everywhere — were besotted with him, and with the whole United States for producing him and Bill Haley and all our other favourites, and with Hollywood and Audrey Hepburn and ballet flat shoes and pirate pants and ponytails and bobbysocks and headscarves tied round the neck at the back *à la* Grace Kelly, and big sunglasses, and open-topped American cars like the Thunderbird. (Cars became very important in the Fifties and Sixties — perhaps because they were the only place you could go to be alone with a boy as we all lived at home then; no wonder there were so many car songs: 'Riding along in my automobile/My baby beside me at the wheel' etc.)

We bought American film magazines and papered our walls with pictures of Elvis, of course, and Natalie Wood, and Tab Hunter and Sal Mineo (incredible that no one has ever heard of any of them nowadays), and, it goes without saying, James Dean, who died in a car crash the year before I went to Paris but lived on in posters above our beds. A complete mis-match with all this Hollywood adulation was the fact that we were also besotted by a completely *French* phenomenon — the singing priest. This was Père Aimé Duval, who was a huge hit in France at that time — he played the guitar and sang gentle songs, which we loved because they seemed very personal and human, and not particularly religious. I found him on YouTube the other day and played one of his songs to Claudia, who groaned, but I hadn't heard his voice for sixty years and suddenly I was seventeen again — it almost made me cry.

# 6

After six months in Paris, I was deemed to be adequately 'finished' (the other girls were staying on for a year) and I had to go back to England for the very un-new-world ritual of being presented at Court.

Had Paris been worth my parents' money? I could speak a bit of French, and I had gained a minuscule amount of confidence, but if I'd been asked to write an inventory of myself then, it wouldn't have added up to much: medium figure, bitten nails, nice legs, small eyes, a plain but animated face, an obsession with open pores (I used to spend hours making face packs from oatmeal and egg white, following recipes in *Woman's Own*, as well as sitting with my elbows in squeezed half lemons because that, apparently, would make them soft and white — as if anyone would ever notice my *elbows*) and, topping all this, thick, curled, dun-coloured hair.

Hair was almost as painful an issue in the Fifties as class. At seventeen we all looked middle-aged because of our uniformly short, permed, and usually brown, hair. The American writer Nora Ephron once said that the most important invention of the twentieth century for women was not feminism or birth control or better living through exercise, it was HAIR DYE. She meant that for the first time in history older women didn't have to go grey. 'In the 1950s only

7 percent of American women dyed their hair; today there are parts of Manhattan and Los Angeles where there are no gray-haired women at all,' she wrote — but in fact, hair dye, or more especially bleach, saved my whole generation of *young* women too, transforming us from mousy frumps into blondes. And we owed another debt to Brigitte Bardot who showed that you could wear your hair long and loose.

Before hair dye and Brigitte Bardot came along to rescue us, the girls in our family could have been straight out of the home-perm advertisement that appeared everywhere at that time. WHICH TWIN HAS THE TONI? it asked, showing identical photographs of identical girls, one supposedly with short, *naturally* curly hair (that was Tessa who was born with curls) and the other with a Toni perm: she represented Moira and me who had poker-straight locks.

Every time any of us went to the hairdresser's in those days, we cried when we came out because they never made us look the way we wanted to. I was wiping away my tears outside a salon in Fleet one day (my permed hair had been arranged into two horn-like curls, one on either side of my forehead) and my mother was lying through her teeth saying, 'It looks really nice, darling,' when a friend passed by and said: 'Glam!' I wanted to throttle her. Moira and I used to joke about this friend, saying that she looked like a horse. We mainly did this to annoy our mother, and one day she fell into the trap and said, 'You girls are so cruel, there is absolutely nothing wrong with that poor girl that soap and water wouldn't put right.' 'Soap and a halter you mean, Mum, ha ha ha,' said Moira, and we both fell about. I think this was my first experience of wit.

At one point I grew my hair to avoid the perms, and wore it in a ponytail or a knot on top of my head like the cancan dancer, La Goulue, in Toulouse-Lautrec's painting (we had all seen John Huston's film *Moulin Rouge* a couple of years earlier). For this style to work it had to be puffy with side wisps, and absolutely not like our mother's friend who had her grey hair scraped severely into a bun. Every time I put my hair up I had to ask Tessa: is it La Goulue or Mum's friend? 'Hmmm,' she'd say, 'it's veering towards Mum's friend, you need to pull the sides out a bit.'

Bra straps were another worry in the Fifties: exposing even the very edge of one was considered sluttish and unacceptable, so bras came in all kinds of convoluted configurations: backless, halter-necked, strapless, with wide-apart straps or close-together straps . . . The idea that forty-plus years later Madonna would liberate women from all these inhibitions by actually wearing a bra with nothing over it, *in public*, on stage, would have shocked us rigid; when I see someone wearing a T-shirt with cut-away armholes that shamelessly expose the straps underneath (e.g., Laure in the TV series *Spiral*), I have to remind myself that it is OK now.

\* \* \*

One of the day students at Mademoiselle Anita's when I was there was a pretty pug-faced girl Henrietta Tiarks, who, like me, had to return to England to be presented at Court — she then married the future Duke of Bedford; another was Tessa Kennedy who caused a huge scandal when she ran away with a young socialite, Dominick Elwes, to be married secretly in Gretna Green. (Even more shocking was the arrest of Caroline, another pupil, for posing in obscene photographs.)

Monika Löwenstein, one of my particular friends, left the school at the end of the year and, soon after, married a Habsburg prince in a Cloth of Gold cape (he not she); they travelled to the reception at her castle in a golden carriage drawn by six white horses — it was even reported in the newspapers in England.

This is the sort of thing (well, not the cape and the carriage and horses, of course) that my parents — and I — hoped would happen to me, but it didn't. When I was sixteen, and first went to finishing school in Paris, I remember thinking that I was SURE to be married within the next ten years, and then, ten years later, being positive that I would be married before the end of my Twenties . . . but I still wasn't. (When I was about twenty-seven I made an agreement with my cousin Nicholas that if neither of us were married by the time we were thirty, we would marry each other, but just before the deadline the cad asked if we could postpone it — and not long after that he married a beautiful dancer.)

Being presented at Court was supposed to help in the process of meeting 'the right person', and my mother's friend Eileen, who had been presented at Court herself, had taken on this duty. I wore a navy-blue princess-line dress and a pink-flowered half-hat of the type Princess Margaret used to wear (she was a bit of a fashion icon in those days). When we arrived at Buckingham Palace, Mum and Dad and Eileen were taken off to sit in the audience, and I was led away to spend what seemed like hours queuing up in an agony of fear with dozens of other debutantes, as we were known, all dressed in similar outfits. Then our names were called out, and one by one, in front of hundreds of spectators, we had to walk across a vast room where the Queen and Prince Philip were seated on thrones, sink into a curtsy in front of each of them, and then walk out the other side. My knees made the most tremendous cracking sound each time I lowered myself down, and Prince Philip smiled slightly. I had been sent for a curtsying lesson to the famous Madame Vacani's dance school (she taught the royal family) — not that I needed it; I could accomplish a flying curtsy while running down a corridor, because at my convent in Farnborough we always had to curtsy when we met Reverend Mother, no matter where we were or what else we were doing.

Afterwards, at the palace, there was a garden party where my parents and I relished the relief of it all being over without any disaster, and tried to look as if this was the sort of thing we did all the time. And not long after this — demonstrating that even the British Establishment recognised that the world was changing — it was announced that, after the following year, 1958, there would be no more presentations at Court.

Sadly — though perhaps it's just as well — there don't seem to be any snaps of me in my presentation outfit, but I do have a photograph that has become a treasure. My mother felt there should be a proper portrait taken to mark my visit to the Palace, and cousin Prue, who was at Guildford Art School then, recommended a fellow student, Tessa Grimshaw, so Mum asked her, and she came to Fleet and did some pictures of me peeking out from behind a tree wearing a Polly Peck dress (they were a good small fashion firm then and not a corporation racked by scandal) — and then, this is the best bit, she went on to become a very famous photographer under her married name, Tessa Traeger. Perhaps my portrait is her very first surviving commission. Mum and Dad also thought my eighteenth birthday, which came in the autumn of that year, should be marked in some way, so they invited three guests to join us for a dinner-dance at the Savoy (poor parents — it must have been sheer hell for them). I had been given the job of selecting the three and, instead of choosing chums from Fleet, I complicated things by suggesting Tim, the son of friends of my parents, whom I hardly knew, but he was tall, dark and handsome. And then, even more oddly, a girl who'd been at my convent — mostly, I think, because I remembered her being quite fat and even uglier than I was and I thought she wouldn't be competition for Tim. But when we all assembled that evening, she had become a slender blonde beauty and she and Tim fell into each other's arms and stayed there all night, leaving me plodding round the dance floor with the second man, who was probably as despondent at the way things had turned out as I was.

Following our presentation, we debutantes 'came out' into society (you'd have to find different words for this now), and 'did the season' — this meant going to other debutantes' balls (my parents couldn't afford one for me, thank goodness) where you met eligible young men who, if they were handsome or rich, were known as Debs' Delights. You also had to go to Ascot races and to Henley Regatta and, ideally, to the May Balls at Cambridge. (The unfortunate man who took me to a May Ball was known by my sisters as the Currant Bun as he had bad spots.) I went to some of these events but with a heavy heart: I felt a complete outsider. Debs' Delights didn't fancy me — I never had to worry about them being Unsafe In Taxis; I didn't fit in, I hated it all, and spent a lot of time in ladies' rooms wishing I could go home. But I felt guilty as well because I knew my parents were spending money they couldn't afford trying to give me 'a good start in life' — it just wasn't a life that I wanted, and there didn't seem to be any other on offer.

It would have been more fun if Anne, my best friend in Fleet, had been sharing all this, but she was not part of that scene; she was doing a secretarial course in Guildford. She met a deb at a party, though. 'What do you do?' Anne asked the deb. 'Oh, I am doing the season in London,' she said. 'What are you doing?' 'I am doing the season in Guildford,' replied Anne, not having a clue what 'doing the season' meant. I was really cheered when she told me this story because it proved there was another, normal life out there somewhere.

Then I started a secretarial course myself, in London. This was more like it. Apart from typing THE QUICK BROWN FOX JUMPS OVER THE LAZY DOG in time to a metronome, and learning shorthand (I can still scrawl 'I am in receipt of your letter' in one contraction, as they are known), we became obsessed with being Beatniks. We smoked like chimneys, outlined our eyes with black pencil, wore a perfume called Evening in Paris, untidied our hair and walked round in bare feet trying to look like the singer Juliette Gréco (I don't know why bare feet came into it; was Juliette known for them?). The sack dress was invented by Balenciaga that year (1957) and Fenwick's store down the road had some cheap copies, but we found you could get the same waistless baggy look by wearing a man's black V-necked sweater back to front over a black pencil skirt. The only problem we had was with lip colour. Real Beatniks in Paris wore very pale pink lipstick — almost white, in fact (frogs' lips, my aunt called them) — and you couldn't get this in England. The first cosmetic company to understand what we wanted was Gala; before that you had to know someone going to France who could get it for you. We Brits were way behind the French then: for instance, the ONLY place in England where you could get your legs waxed in those days was Elizabeth Arden in Bond Street, which cost a fortune. (On the other hand, as we observed on our holidays, it took longer in France for proper lavatory paper to become available: they had cut up newspapers threaded on string for years.)

★   ★   ★

I qualified as a secretary when I was seventeen and found a cosy job working for three middle-aged ladies who ran an organisation called the Dominions Fellowship Trust; my salary was five pounds a week. I was the junior to an elderly, gloomy spinster secretary — one of my jobs was to buy the stamps at the post office every week, so one day, in an effort to cheer her up, I brought back the biggest, prettiest new-issue Christmas stamps. 'Look, Miss Porcheron,' I chirped, 'such lovely stamps!' She glanced at them and groaned. 'Oh no,' she said glumly, 'there's so much more to lick.'

The Dominions Fellowship Trust office was just off Sloane Square, by the side of Peter Jones, which was great as my parents and friends could come and chat to me through my window. The boss was called Miss Macdonald of Sleat (pronounced Slate); she was very grand and had been a childhood friend of the Queen Mother. What the Trust did was to look after students from the Commonwealth coming to study, often on scholarships, in the UK. We had, for instance, to find them places to stay during the holidays if they couldn't go home. This involved endless letters to potential hostesses and students, which I would type and send off — quite often in the wrong envelopes, so that I had to spend a good deal of time standing by the pillar box on the pavement outside the office praying that the postman would come and give me back my letters because otherwise disaster would strike. 'Dear Lady Fotherington, thank you so much for offering to take Njogo Ceesay for the Christmas holidays. He is twenty-four years old, very dark and a little unusual to look at because of the tribal scars on his cheeks, but he has a heart of gold, is an excellent student and I am sure you will find him a perfect guest' would be en route to Mr Ceesay, and 'Dear Mr Ceesay, I am delighted to tell you that Lady Fotherington has kindly agreed to host you for the Christmas holidays. She is a very large lady with unusual blue hair and you might find her intimidating at first, but she had a heart of gold, etc., etc.' was on its way to Lady Fotherington.

I loved the postman because he always let me go through the letters to find mine, even though it was against all the rules. He used to call me his Little Ray of Sunshine.

⋆　⋆　⋆

Eighteen months later, I left my old ladies and went to work as a typist at Westminster Press Provincial Newspapers's office in London. I didn't want to work on a paper, I had no ambition to become a journalist ('Men don't like career girls'), but Moira, who was on the *Sunday Times* by then, had begun her own successful newspaper career at Westminster Press as a temp (which is probably why I was offered the job) and she persuaded me to make the move. I worked for the same boss as she had — a wonderful woman with nicotine-stained hair and fingers, called Margaret Pierce, who put together daily women's pages, including fashion articles, which were sent out to the provincial papers in 'our' group, the main one being the *Northern Echo* of Darlington. I was happy in the typing pool with a couple of new friends, doing letters, and Margaret would occasionally pluck me out and get me to work with her on fashion captions or choosing photographs.

And then a vacancy came up for a fashion assistant at the *Daily Express* and Margaret and Moira urged me to apply. I wished I hadn't when I got there. My boss was Jill Butterfield, aka the Golden Girl of Fleet Street, whose photo appeared on the sides of London buses and I found her — and everyone else for that matter — utterly terrifying. My biggest shock was the swearing — my parents never swore (strangely, I happened to be watching the television with them when Kenneth Tynan said the F-word on it for the very first time; none of us made any comment, it might never have happened). The only person who took any notice of me was the cartoonist Artie — he was short and plump and half-Indian, I think, and whenever there was a particularly gruesome murder, everyone used to tease him by shouting out, 'Where were you yesterday, Artie?' and Artie would look guilty.

I don't think I dared raise my eyes far off the floor of the *Express* for most of the time I was there, though I did eventually make a lifelong friend in my protector and ally against the Golden Girl: Meriel McCooey, who was the senior fashion assistant. My job was mostly to telephone manufacturers and call in clothes that the Golden Girl had seen at fashion shows and wanted to feature on her pages, and then to help Meriel carry them to the studios where she had arranged for them to be photographed. And I was supposed to contribute IDEAS at brain-storming sessions which were agony because I never had any, and even if I had, I would have been too shy of being laughed at to mention them.

It's hard to imagine now, but the *Daily Express* was *the* cutting-edge newspaper at that time. It had a brilliant associate editor, Harold Keeble, who understood the importance of layout, and the paper employed two legendary art directors: Ray Hawkey, who went on to the *Observer* (he also designed Len Deighton's state-of-the art book covers as well as the first paperback James Bonds), and Michael Rand, who became art director of the *Sunday Times* and designer of its colour magazine — the first one published in Britain. This meant that on our fashion pages the photographs were used bigger and more dramatically than in any other paper — or even in most magazines — so all the best photographers were keen to work for us.

Our main fashion photographer was the legendary John French — a tall, thin, elegant man in a grey suit who looked exactly like a crane (the bird sort). He never actually took a photograph himself but had young male assistants who, when John had posed the model girl to his liking and called out 'STILL!' in his grand camp voice, pressed the button to snap the picture.

John French was generous and encouraged these assistants in their own careers, and nearly all of them went on to great things — particularly David Bailey, of course. I often met him at the John French studio when I was carrying clothes in to be photographed; we were almost the same age (he was twenty-two, I was twenty) but I was nervous of him as I had never met anyone like this cocky, confident, energetic, handsome lad in a black leather jacket with an irreverent sense of humour. (''Hello,' he lied' was a favourite greeting of his that still makes me laugh.)

Years later he had to take a portrait of me and, to make me relax and forget my nerves, he threatened to undo the zip of his flies — I can't say that made me relax exactly, but it did make me scream. After he had joined *Vogue* and become famous, a story went round about Bailey and a model who was considered a bit dim; I have no idea whether it is true. The tale goes that the model was posing for him at the *Vogue* studios and he was making the usual encouraging remarks: 'Great, great. Wonderful. Great.

Hold that pose, darlin' . . . ' Then he walked out of the studio and caught a plane to Paris where he had lunch, and when he got back to *Vogue* hours later, the model said, 'I haven't moved!'

Back at the *Express*, at John French's suggestion, Bailey, who had just gone independent, brought his own portfolio in to show the art director. Almost immediately it got lost but was eventually found under a carpet in Harold Keeble's office — perhaps Bailey's life would have been different if it hadn't turned up. He was booked for a sitting (as they were known in those days, rather than 'shoots') at the studio in Shepherd Market where he was working then; it was for a fashion feature being organised by Meriel called 'Autumn Girl'. The picture they took became an iconic one — it was, apparently, the reason *Vogue* magazine signed up Bailey, which led him to fame and fortune. I say 'they' took, because Meriel was an inspired stylist and it was she who chose the clothes and the model, Paulene Stone, and took the stuffed squirrel to the studio (squirrels = autumn). Bailey photographed Paulene kneeling, as if talking to the squirrel, instead of standing facing the camera in the usual model stance of that time; it was a wonderful picture — the *Express* used it across the top half of a page — and nothing in fashion photography was ever the same again. In fact it got quite silly, with photographers and fashion editors vying with each other to do something ever more 'different'. Photographer John Cowan pictured models hang-gliding or was it parachuting, I can't remember. Molly Parkin at *Nova* had

151

them posing in bed together, pretending to be lesbians, as well as girls in white dresses and real diamonds on top of a mountain in real snow. My own personal best came later, when I had moved to the *Sunday Times*: I hired a horse, A LIVE HORSE, and took it in a lift up to the photographer Barry Warner's studio in Kensington, where we photographed a model sitting on it wearing a selection of leather 'riding' boots (these were the point of my fashion story). The art department at the *Sunday Times* cut the picture so that you could hardly see the horse — it could almost have been a patch of paint daubed on to the background paper, and I'd gone to all that trouble . . .

Almost as much trouble as when (once again for the *Sunday Times*) I decided to photograph a copy of one of Yves Saint Laurent's sequined dresses on a trapeze artist. I contacted Bertram Mills Circus (still going strong in those days) and was put in touch with a charming member of the family, Cyril Mills, who was quite enthusiastic about the idea and persuaded their own real trapeze star, Shirley Fossett, to dress up in the glittery garment and do her high-flying act — spinning in mid-air from her teeth — for the photographer Norman Eales. He did a dazzling picture of her whirling round in space, but I don't have even an old yellowed newspaper cutting of it now. Norman Eales died many years ago, but I wonder if this fantastic image still exists somewhere: I hope so. We were all so careless of our fashion pictures then, just chucking them in the dustbin when the drawers of the layout table got too full.

★　★　★

In the giant open-plan office at the *Daily Express*, which had banners strung across it saying ACCURACY FIRST LAST AND ALWAYS and GET IT IN YOUR FIRST LINE, GET IT IN YOUR HEADLINE AND IN PICTURES MOST OF ALL, I sat next to the famous cartoonist Osbert Lancaster. He was about fifty and looked exactly like an upper-class gentleman from one of his own cartoons — immaculately dressed in pinstriped suits, with a flamboyant moustache, and a cigarette held elegantly between his fingers. He used to come into the office fairly late, do his cartoon for next day, and then leave. Sometimes I was allowed a say in what his main character, Maudie Littlehampton, wore — a suit, a dress, spots or stripes, etc. Was it this that encouraged me to invite him for drinks at my flat? Otherwise what on earth possessed me to do such a thing? Was I unwittingly social climbing? (No one talks about social climbing these days, it's known as 'networking' and is perfectly respectable.) I was such a weird mixture of recklessness and extreme timidity. Fifty-five years later, writing this, I still feel horrified at the thought of my invitation, remembering how, having issued it, I was overcome by total panic. I couldn't think of anyone to invite with him, so in utter desperation I got a group of girlfriends from my secretarial schooldays to come. They were thrilled to meet the great man, and sat at his feet looking at him adoringly all evening. I think that he might even have enjoyed himself.

A working day at the *Daily Express* didn't end when you went home in the evenings: about three times a week the phone would ring and it would be someone at the office wanting you to go back in to a write a caption for a picture of the Queen opening a school, or a film star on the red carpet at a première in Leicester Square or, basically, any photograph involving a woman and clothes or hats. They could easily have done the captions themselves — perhaps they just liked torturing us.

During the summer of the year I was at the *Express*, I was asked by someone on the William Hickey page (the gossip column) to give them a hand with their annual Ladies' Day at Ascot races story. 'This is what I'd like you to do,' the journalist instructed me. 'Once you're there, try and spot a celebrity and then follow him or her round for the rest of the afternoon and note down everyone they speak to, what they are wearing, and so on.' I was incredibly lucky — the moment I arrived I spotted the Aga Khan and followed his handsome figure all afternoon. Sure enough, he was always talking to someone famous — of course, I said to myself, keeping a discreet distance so he wouldn't realise I was stalking him, his friends *would* all be celebrities like him. I was thrilled at the brilliant job I was doing, jotting everything down in my notebook like a real reporter, and then I went back to London to hand in my notes and accept lavish praise. To my puzzlement, as I walked into the office, the first person I saw was the 'Aga Khan' ... who, it turned out, was Peter Sen, a British-Indian reporter working on the William Hickey column whom I hadn't come across at the paper before. Of course he was talking to all the famous people at Ascot because he was doing the job I thought I was doing.

*   *   *

I was given the task of looking after a woman who'd won a fashion competition we had run on our pages. The prize was a free couture outfit, plus the accessories that went with it, and a day in London visiting the couturier — John Cavanagh — to choose it all and be measured and so on. The Golden Girl had decided in advance that the winner had to have a little black dress because the fashion page was going to offer a paper pattern of the garment that was chosen, and she wanted this to be a party frock. The winner, poor nice Mrs X (I can't remember her name), lived in the country, and all she wanted was a useful but pretty woollen suit and some smart everyday shoes and matching handbag, but she was made to have the little black dress instead, and then of course the accessories that went with it. I was sad about her disappointment, but I felt even more like a traitor when, later on, I was asked by the picture desk to book a *pretend* fashion sitting with a model, April Ashley, who, one of the news reporters had discovered, had only recently been a MAN. 'Get her to pull her skirt up her thighs, make her cross her legs, get a shot of her cleavage,' they instructed me. I just wanted to cry because April Ashley was charming, and really believed she was modelling for a fashion picture and not a lurid story about her sex change.

Michael Parkinson was on the sports desk at the *Express* when I first went there; he was more or less unknown then, and was always kind to Meriel and me, which is why, ages later, after I'd joined the *Sunday Times* and had been roped into helping with a What Famous People Want in Their Stocking story (an annual newspaper Christmas favourite), I rang Parky, now a 'celebrity', to ask him the question. 'I can't believe you are still doing this kind of crap, Brigid,' he said, and I remembered that slight feeling of shame I always had at the *Express*.

One of my weirdest experiences there had nothing to do with journalism: it was my first and only experience of SMOG. No one who has not experienced smog can imagine what it was like: I stepped out of the famous black-glass *Express* building in Fleet Street and seemingly into oblivion — a dense white cloud through which you could see nothing. There was a deathly silence, no vehicle could move, so it was a question of walking home. It can't be that difficult, I thought, even in this fog — but I ended up, not in Sloane Square where I had been headed, but on the other side of Waterloo Bridge: I had not even known as I walked, peering into the enveloping blankness, that I had crossed over the Thames. The only thing since that has felt anything like that evening was Antony Gormley's exhibition *Blind Light* at the Hayward Gallery in 2007, in which he put 'smog' in large glass boxes that visitors had to try and make their way through — you could see that people were unnerved by the experience.

★   ★   ★

Not long before I left the *Express*, I came across a company called Nylons Unlimited which sold stockings not in pairs, but in threes. We all wore stockings then, and when they laddered you were left with one that didn't match any others, so this seemed like a good idea, and I mentioned it to the Golden Girl and she said, 'Why don't you write the story yourself?' Panic-stricken, I wrote and rewrote my two paragraphs about fifty times and then handed them in; my first line went something like: 'In the middle of the night John Jones [I don't recall his real name] leapt out of bed with a really good idea . . . ' This was greeted with loud guffaws by everyone, and the Golden Girl made a copy of my little article to pass round the office for a laugh. I felt a complete fool.

I thought of this some time ago when I happened to read the obituary of someone called Julian Thompson who had been chairman of Sotheby's, as well as its distinguished Chinese porcelain expert. He joined the company aged eighteen and the first thing he did was to drop a stack of priceless Chinese *famille rose* plates he was carrying, which broke into a million pieces.

157

That was much worse than my writing debut — but he went on to be head of the firm, and I went on to be a Young Meteor; so, if you are starting out on a career, making mistakes and blunders, and reading this, be cheered.

★ ★ ★

After about a year of feeling like a fish out of water at the *Express*, I was offered a job as fashion assistant on the *Sunday Times* (where Moira was still working) and I left the black-glass building on Fleet Street for good — though it never quite left me. Even now, all these decades later, when I hear a telephone ringing in the early evening — even if I am somewhere like Kazakhstan — my first reaction is a sinking heart because I think I am going to be called back to the office to write a fashion caption.

# 7

While I did my secretarial course I had
commuted to London every day and since I was
often running late I would sometimes have to
buy my ticket at the end of my journey: Waterloo.
One day there, instead of asking for a ticket from
Fleet, I had the bright idea of saying I'd come
from Woking which was nearer and cheaper
— whereupon the man at the barrier said, 'When
you caught the train at Woking, did you have to
cross the bridge to get to your platform?' My jaw
dropped, I couldn't answer the question; I stood
there with my mouth gaping and then I burst
into tears and said, 'It's all a lie, I've come from
Fleet.' I confessed to Mum and Dad that evening
what had happened, and they told me the story
of Professor Joad, an immensely celebrated
philosopher and radio personality who caused
one of the biggest scandals of their era when, in
1948, he dodged his rail fare (also on a Waterloo
train), was caught, fined (two pounds), sacked by
the BBC and became a ruined man. I never
dared cheat again.

Once I started work at the *Daily Express*, I
went to live with Moira at first, and then moved
into another flat which I shared with a girlfriend,
Margaret, in Chelsea, but I nearly always went
home for the weekends. Almost every time I did
this journey I would forget my suitcase on the
train and have to run to the stationmaster in

Fleet and ask him to phone the next stop down the line, Hook, and ask them to take it off. 'Look, 'Ook,' he'd say, endearingly, each time he rang them. Then my father and I would have to do a five-mile detour to Hook on the way home. I must have driven my parents mad. Luckily they never knew about my worst misadventure. My friends in Fleet decided to organise a jolly picnic one Saturday; for some reason, I was not coming home on that Friday night, but I said I would come down by train next morning and join them.

'No, no,' they replied. 'We know you — you'll miss the train, you will never be in Fleet in time, you'll hold us up and ruin everything . . . '

'I *promise* I'll be there,' I pledged. 'You'll see, I won't let you down, I will be there.'

'OK,' they said, 'but if you are late, we are going on without you.'

The Saturday came and I missed the train. In utter panic and desperation I hailed a taxi — A LONDON BLACK CAB — and asked him to drive me to Fleet. We arrived at the station (the rendezvous) at the same time as the train I would have caught if I had simply stayed at Waterloo. My friends had gone, the taxi (I paid by cheque) cost all my savings. I didn't dare tell my parents what I had done; I just went back to London with the taxi-driver, crying, and told them the picnic had been cancelled. My friends never knew I'd come; they thought I'd just stood them up.

\* \* \*

Weekends in Fleet couldn't have been more different from life in London — they seemed to revolve around horses (not that we ourselves had a horse, or even knew anyone with one). There were point-to-points (races) on Saturdays at a place called Tweseldown somewhere near Aldershot, and hunt balls. My memories of hunt balls could send me into a downward spiral right now: cold damp evenings freezing to death in a hideous pale-blue-tulle party frock with a tweed overcoat on top, scared stiff at being driven by some youth who had not long passed his driving test (and would probably have lots to drink in the course of the evening) to the Hog's Back Hotel or wherever the party was, and back.

One particular evening stands out. On the way to the ball in a car full of young people, I decided I should touch up my lipstick. Being shy about doing this in public, I didn't take out a mirror but fumbled around in my bag until my fingers felt the lipstick tube, and then I went over my lips boldly enough to last all evening. When we arrived, I went in smiling and greeting friends but got an odd, embarrassed response. What was wrong? I went into the cloakroom to leave my coat, glanced in the mirror — and saw with horror that my lips were bright turquoise-blue (eyeliner came in lipstick-like tubes in those days; my fingers had settled on the wrong little cylinder). It's impossible to understand now how shocking blue lips were, back in the Fifties — let alone in that staid venue; I like to imagine that perhaps Sid Vicious was there as a young guest

161

or waiter that evening and that my lips inspired Punk.

At hunt balls there was a dance called the Paul Jones, designed to discomfort not-particularly-attractive young women. In a Paul Jones, all the young men form a big circle and revolve around an inner circle made up of all the girls. The men and women are facing each other, and when the music stops, they must dance with the person they find themselves opposite. It should have been entertaining, but you were never *exactly* opposite someone when the music stopped, and in my experience, the men who should have danced with me usually made a dive for the girls on either side. (Step forward, offender Jeremy Quinlan!) To be fair, I expect it was all just as unnerving for young men — years before, when my brother went to his first hunt ball, the girl he was dancing with suddenly slapped him on the shoulder and said, 'I'll be man now.'

Hunt balls went on, I suppose — and probably still do — but pretty soon I could forget about them because the New World arrived in our neighbourhood. The Officers' Club in nearby Aldershot (still 'Home of the British Army' in those days) introduced Rock and Roll evenings. I could rock and roll far better than I could waltz or foxtrot, and in my circular felt skirt (made by Moira who was trying to earn extra money by sewing these for friends) with a paper nylon petticoat underneath to puff it out, and my wide cinched-in belt and Diana Dors bosom (i.e., two ice-cream cones) under a tight sweater, I was suddenly in my element. Nearly all the girls in

Fleet in my day met our first boyfriends there — I was madly in love with two young officers, not at the same time of course, but one after the other; they were both from the Parachute Regiment. My sisters called me the ParaPet. I could have become engaged to one of them but, extraordinarily, was sensible enough not to take that step.

# 8

My career on the fashion pages of the *Sunday Times* hardly needs explaining if you have seen the film *The Devil Wears Prada*. My boss, an American called Ernestine Carter, was the terrifying editor played by Meryl Streep, though she looked entirely different. Mrs Carter was tiny, with a black velvet bow or a small Jacqueline Kennedy-type pillbox hat on short, greying curly hair; her clothes were simple and immaculate (again, like Mrs Kennedy's) and she wore low-heeled pumps in patent leather. I can't really put my finger on why she was so scary; she had odd, flecked browny-green eyes, but it wasn't them that made your stomach turn over if she looked at you; I think there are just some people in the world who instil fear. Mademoiselle Anita in Paris was one, and Mrs Carter was another — and she was similar to Mademoiselle Anita in so far as no one seemed to know anything about her past or her background in the US, or how she got to be at the *Sunday Times*; the only thing we knew about her is that she was married to the Old Etonian antiquarian book expert at Sotheby's.

I worked for her for years, went on press trips abroad with her — once all the way to Hong Kong — but I never called her anything except Mrs Carter, and though I became quite fond of her, I never lost my fear. Years after I had left the

164

newspaper world, married AW, gone abroad and had children, I happened to be in London when she died, and the *Sunday Times* asked me to write her obituary. I was horrified, it was like lesé-majesty, I couldn't possibly do it, but it turned out to be surprisingly easy, and I came to the conclusion that she was dictating it herself, from above.

One of Mrs Carter's many quirks was a belief that people who wrote to newspapers were mad, and that mad people couldn't spell — and the weird thing is that she was often right about the spelling. Her letters back to her readers would go something like: 'Dear Mrs Throgmorton. Thank you for your letter, I would have taken your criticisms more seriously had you not written 'fashion' with two s's.'

(I myself was to continue to put letters in the wrong envelopes; most embarrassingly when I replied to a reader who wanted to know what to do about her hairy legs, and put my letter in an envelope addressed to another woman who had complained about a special-offer dress she had bought from us being so transparent that her black shirt showed through. The result was that the hairy-legged reader got advice suggesting she lined her dress so 'the black' didn't show through, and the transparent-dress reader got a letter suggesting she wax her hairy legs.)

My main job on the *Sunday Times* was to assist the journalist doing the 'Young Grown-Ups' column (the very name of the column tells you what 'young' fashions were like then), and I also had to help Mrs Carter's assistant organise the photographs for the main fashion page. Both of these jobs involved doing almost exactly what I had done at the *Daily Express* — ordering in clothes and taking them to the studios to be photographed — but the really good part was that my beloved sister Moira was there in the same office (writing features).

Then an extraordinary thing happened — it was like another, smaller Hollywood film within the main *Devil Wears Prada* one. The woman I was assisting was expecting a baby, and one morning something began to go wrong and her doctor told her to go home and rest and not to even think of going back to the office for the remainder of her pregnancy.

There was no one else to do her job and so it fell to me to get her column to press that week, and start working on another one for the following Sunday. I remember I wrote about accessories made of cork (probably because I'd managed to think up what I imagined was a snappy headline: 'Corking Good Fun!' or 'What a Corker!' — I can't now recall what I called the feature) and the text was pretty much as dire as the story I had done on the *Daily Express*. But somehow the weeks went by and no replacement was found for me, and so I simply segued into being the editor of the Young Fashion page — as we now decided to call it because girls were not dressing like Young Grown-Ups any more.

What an incredible piece of luck for me — and it was luck I could really enjoy because my previous boss's pregnancy went well and her baby was safely delivered. To be truthful, none of it had anything much to do with my ability; it was just that I happened to be a person of the *right age* in the right place at the right time. I suppose the only thing you could say in my favour was that I accepted the challenge and gave the job my best shot — and, all of a sudden, on my own, I began to get the ideas I had never managed to come up with on the *Express*.

★   ★   ★

Socially, though, I was still pathetically naive and extremely shy but with an impulsive streak — a combination that tended to land me in awkward situations. Some of them wouldn't have happened if only we'd had mobile phones. This was one: Martin, my boyfriend at the time (he worked in the advertising department of the *Sunday Times*), was going to stay with friends in Ibiza and asked me to go with him. I couldn't because I had work to do over the bank holiday weekend, so he wrote down the address — it was all in Spanish — in case I changed my mind, and left. I managed to finish my work sooner than expected, so I sent Martin a telegram (we still had them in those days), saying I was on my way, and giving the flight details. My plane arrived in Ibiza very early in the morning so I was not completely surprised that there was no one there to meet me. They'll be along at a more civilised time, I thought to myself, maybe eight or eight thirty am, but no one had come by ten so I asked a taxi to take me to the address on the piece of paper. When we arrived, however, it wasn't a private house, but a villa agency, a place that sold and let accommodation. I didn't know the surname of Martin's friends — and without that the agency couldn't identify or locate them. As I stood there, dazed by the awfulness of travelling all this way and spending all that money for nothing, the agency man said, 'Oh, we have a telegram, maybe it is from you? It has no name on it so we couldn't deliver it,' and he produced the telegram I'd sent Martin — which meant that no one was even aware I was coming. I knew there was a flight back to London that evening and I had five pounds in my pocket, so I decided to go and get something to eat at a café which Martin and I had been to on a previous holiday and try to while away a few hours there before catching the flight home again. Through my tears I told the agency man my plan and then went and sat, despairing, in the café (the English couple who ran it were much less nice to me when they knew I only had five pounds than they had been the year before when I'd had Martin and more money) where I prayed for a miracle. It happened about an hour later: Martin and his friends drove up in their car . . .

For the first time in a week they had been to the agency to see if there was any post, been shown my telegram and told where I'd gone — and here they were! This story had a happy ending but there would have been no unhappiness at all if we'd all been able to contact each other on mobile phones.

And mobile phones might have helped prevent the embarrassing restaurant débâcle which happened around the same time. This came about when an elegant older woman I met at a party invited me to lunch with her at 'Laze-Ay'. I hadn't a clue where or what that was but I didn't dare ask — I thought I would find out from Moira on the morning of the date. But when the day came (I remember it was a Monday), Moira was not in the office for some reason and no one else had any idea what Laze-Ay was. (Had we had mobile phones I could have rung her and she would have known.)

With a growing feeling of doom, I looked it up in the phone book, but the only name I could find that sounded anything like 'Laze-Ay' — and then only if you said it with a French accent — was a restaurant in Soho called Lezzet's. There was nothing else, so I decided that must be it. I told my assistant where I was going and set off — only to discover when I arrived that Lezzet's was a dingy Turkish eatery into which I knew my elegant lady would never ever set her toe, let alone foot. I found a phone and rang my assistant to say that, if my lunch date called, for God's sake not to reveal where I had gone — but it was too late, she'd already telephoned, been given the address and was on her way to meet me in a taxi. There was no way to stop her, so I had to wait outside Lezzet's for the awful moment when she would arrive, see the greasy-spoon restaurant and realise that I was a complete idiot: all of which duly happened before she told her taxi to take us both to Les Ambassadeurs — one of the smartest clubs in London, nicknamed Les A by the rich and famous. We had an awkward, late lunch, and then I never saw her again.

But mobile phones would not have prevented some of the other cringe-making episodes in my life. I met a rather posh man at this time, quite a lot older than me, and was invited to stay with his sister and her husband for a weekend. My parents were thrilled — he was not a paratrooper; his mother had a title and lived in a castle; they could see their original plan for my 'suitable' marriage and comfortable future being resurrected before their eyes. His sister had a double-barrelled name — lots of people seemed to have them in those days: Muspratt-Williams, Tennyson-d'Eyncourt, Hamilton-Fleming, Money-Coutts; and shops did too: Marshall & Snelgrove, Swan & Edgar, Dickins & Jones, Debenham & Freebody; now I barely know a person or a shop with double names.

I felt very ill at ease staying with these grand-sounding people and desperately wanted to go home, but though I racked my brains I couldn't think of an excuse to leave — until on the Sunday morning it came to me: I would say that I had to go to confession; they were Catholics, was my reasoning, they would understand. So, after breakfast, when plans for the day were being discussed, I suddenly said, 'I am afraid I have to leave now to go to confession.' '*Confession?*' they said in unison, looking astonished. 'Yes,' I said, 'I'm afraid so, I must leave straight away,' and I went to collect my things. They must have thought I was raving mad; my mother was furious when I turned up. For non-Catholics I should explain that you would only ever *have* to go to confession if you had done something really bad like murdering someone.

The older man was understanding; he drove me home and was not put off by my peculiar behaviour — we very nearly got engaged, but marrying him would have meant living in South America, and in the end I couldn't go through with it. Mum didn't speak to me for months.

That was also the year I was sick in my handbag at a party — one given by the Golden Girl of all people. I blame my waspie — a 'waspie' was a Fifties corset that went around your middle; it was boned, and you (or preferably someone else) had to lace it up very, very tightly to give yourself a tiny waist — just like Scarlett O'Hara in *Gone with the Wind*.

It was warm, and halfway through the evening I knew I was going to be sick. I rushed upstairs to the loo but there was someone in it; I looked out of the window, but couples were standing chatting outside, including the Golden Girl; the wastepaper basket on the landing was lined in pretty chintz; there was absolutely NOWHERE to throw up, so I opened my bag and was sick into that. (We all had big square patent-leather handbags in those days.) The worst part about this story is that Moira and her friends took me on out to a restaurant after the party — I wasn't allowed to refuse — so I had to carry my burden around London all evening.

Two years later something similar happened when I went to my assistant Edwina's twenty-first-birthday costume party dressed as Mary,

Queen of Scots. There was a medieval dinner first, at which mead was served, and then the revels moved on to a boat on the Thames. What with a surfeit of mead and the rocking of the boat, I very soon had to go to the ladies', and then, having been heard vomiting in the loo by everyone, I didn't dare come out of the cubicle — it was *my assistant's* party after all — so I stayed there, sitting on the lid, half the night, listening to people saying, 'Have you seen Brigid? She seems to have disappeared,' after which, when most of the guests had apparently left, I crept off the boat and fled along the Embankment to find a taxi. I sometimes wonder if anyone saw me and thought I was a ghost; it's not every day you see a young woman in a long black velvet dress with a white ruff and a little heart-shaped headdress wandering round by the river in the middle of the night.

I am so glad that I am not young any more.

# 9

I was twenty-one in 1961 when I became the Young Fashion editor. Only a few months before, on the *Express*, there didn't seem to be many young people involved in fashion at all, and the clothes we featured were by nameless designers working for big companies — Horrockses, Susan Small, Berkertex, Reldan, etc. — but now, almost literally overnight it seemed, there was a significant number of us, all roughly the same age, and working in different areas of the fashion business, from designing to writing, to photography, to modelling, to hairdressing. How on earth did this happen? It reminds me of something Colin Thubron once said about Russia — that during the Communist regime the only females you saw in the Soviet Union were old and sour-faced, but now every woman there is a beauty; where were the beauties in the old days, he wondered, and where are the sour-faced ones now?

We were practically children: Jean Shrimpton was eighteen, just out of the Lucie Clayton modelling school; so was her friend and fellow model Celia Hammond, as well as Paulene Stone who had won a *Woman's Own* model-girl competition. Marit Allen, a young journalist who was making a big name for herself on *Queen* magazine (she later did the Young Idea pages in *Vogue*), was nineteen and David Bailey was twenty-three, the same age as many of the new designers, most of them graduates from the Royal College of Art where Janey Ironside was the professor of fashion: Marion Foale and Sally Tuffin, James Wedge, Gerald McCann, Roger Nelson and John Bates as Jean Varon. (Marit Allen chose John Bates to design her wedding dress which is owned by the V&A now and was part of the museum's *Bridal Dresses* exhibition a couple of years ago.) Mrs Carter had, warily, not opened her arms to the young designers, but it was said that she liked John Bates the moment she met him because he was wearing an Old Etonian tie — it never occurred to her that he had bought it in a charity shop.

At twenty-six, Mary Quant was a tiny bit older than most of us, and she had already opened her two hugely influential Bazaar shops. Vidal Sassoon, responsible for the huge revolution in hairdressing that was also taking place at the time (no more perms, no more 'horns' curling on the forehead), was thirty-two (he'd already had other careers, including fighting for the Israeli Army in 1948), and so was Jean Muir who was just leaving Jaeger (where she had designed the Young Jaeger range) to set up her own business, Jane & Jane, later Jean Muir.

Over in the parallel world of furniture and 'living', Terence Conran, thirty in 1961, was doing for interiors what the young fashion stars were doing for clothes: his Habitat store, which opened in 1964, a little further down the King's Road from Mary Quant's first Bazaar boutique, meant that for the very first time there were household furnishings especially designed with young people's taste — and budgets — in mind. We no longer had to make lamps out of Mateus Rosé or Chianti bottles with straw bottoms to show how cool we were.

Fifty years later, in 2014, David Bailey and Terence Conran helped me to recommend Mary Quant for a damehood. She had long ago received the OBE but, whereas less influential designers like Zandra Rhodes (whom I love and admire) and Vivienne Westwood had been made dames since, Mary Quant — by far the most important British designer in the second part of the twentieth century — had somehow missed out. The sad part was that by the time her damehood was announced, Mary was beginning to suffer from dementia — and so, it seemed, were the newspapers: barely a single one followed up the story, and the BBC World Service announced 'Mary Quant joins the list of *Welsh* honoured today,' as though being Welsh was her claim to fame. If ever one was needed, this was a salutary lesson in the fragility of fame; society's memory is very short.

★　★　★

My new job as Young Fashion editor was to see all the young designers' collections and choose the clothes I liked, or that fitted my 'story', and then get them photographed for my space which covered the top half of a page each week.

In my early days at the *Sunday Times*, I nearly always chose David Bailey as my photographer (I was at ease with him by now) and Jean Shrimpton as my model. There were no make-up artists and hairdressers involved then — Jean did her own face and hair — so there were just the three of us and we could get the pictures done in no time at all. Occasionally we photographed the clothes outside the studio — once in the Establishment, a nightclub being opened by Peter Cook after the success of his hilarious satirical revue *Beyond the Fringe* (with Alan Bennett, Dudley Moore and Jonathan Miller) which had taken London by storm the previous year. The builders were running late and there were cables and paint pots and planks all over the place, and Peter Cook was really irritated by us being there as well, and swore a lot.

Mostly we photographed in Studio 5 in Shepherd Market, or, later, in the studios at *Vogue* magazine, or later still in Bailey's house, which was painted black inside and was where he kept his pet parrots.

The other part of my job was still helping to organise the photographs for Ernestine Carter's page — this was much less fun as she chose the clothes and I didn't usually like them, but I dutifully carted them off to be photographed, and did my best. When the contact sheets of her pictures came into the office from the photographers, she used to call me in while she looked at them through a magnifying glass, then she'd say: 'Dear girl' (she called all her staff 'dear girl' or 'dearie', and had a secret ambition, she once confided in me, to see us all dressed in the same black dresses with white collars), 'dear girl, which picture do you like here?' 'I like that one, Mrs Carter,' I would say, pointing, and every time she would say, 'Do you? How odd, this one here is much better,' and that is the picture that would get used.

(Another thing about Mrs Carter is that she would give us seemingly generous Christmas presents: lavish sets of beauty products. It was only when we opened the boxes and delved inside that we'd find a card from Helena Rubinstein or Elizabeth Arden or Estée Lauder to Mrs Carter personally, wishing her a happy Christmas.)

\* \* \*

In the Fifties we all made our own clothes because we could never find what we wanted in the shops. Back home in Fleet there was almost always a length of fabric on the dining-room table with a Simplicity or Butterick or Vogue paper pattern pinned to it, waiting to be cut out by Moira or Tessa or me. If things went wrong with our sewing, we'd say to each other, 'Don't worry, it'll be all right when it's ironed,' and it usually was. (When Paulene Stone won the *Woman's Own* model competition, part of the prize was an outfit from Fenwick's but, since she and her mother had always made her clothes, they had no idea what size she was.)

This is exactly what the newly emerging young designers were doing — they were basically making the clothes that they wanted to wear *themselves* or see their women friends in. Mary

177

Quant had been the first to do this: selling her 'own' clothes — exactly like the ones she wore herself — in her Bazaar boutiques. I remember coveting a grey flannel suit with a box-pleated skirt that was in the window in the King's Road shop, but not being able to afford it — and then a friend of mine got a job in Mary Quant's workroom and she made it for me at half the price. (One of Mary's most successful ideas was to use fabrics that had never before been seen in women's fashion: grey flannel, for instance, traditionally a cloth for men's trousers and suits; or gingham, more commonly found in curtains and tablecloths; or Liberty printed lawn, traditionally a choice for children's clothes.)

There was one other boutique in Chelsea, run by Kiki Byrne who had worked for Mary; these (and occasionally Fenwick's) were about the only places selling clothes that tempted girls of my age — and they were way too expensive for most of us.

Then, in 1961, the fashion revolution really took off: Martin Moss, an enlightened managing director of Woollands, the department store which once stood next to Harvey Nichols in Knightsbridge (it was pulled down to make way for the Sheraton Park Tower hotel in 1969), hired a young buyer called Vanessa Denza and together they opened the 21 Shop to celebrate the new young designers and sell their clothes — including the first modern trouser suit which was made by Foale and Tuffin — at prices young women could (almost) afford. Customers poured in — so many that there were queues outside;

Vanessa Denza said it was like a dam bursting.

There was a freshness and an excitement in the air: in the Sixties we began to think we could do anything — and when President and Mrs Kennedy, with their glamorous, Camelot, new-kind-of-leader aura, visited London that year, they seemed to be a part of it, and I joined the crowds waiting for hours in the Mall to watch them flash past, dazzlingly, on their way to dine with the Queen at Buckingham Palace.

Two and a half years later I was on my way back to my flat in Battersea from a press trip to Oslo, when I was stopped outside the main door of our block by Mr Mead, who lived on the ground floor and was a sort of scruffy, self-appointed porter; he told me President Kennedy had been murdered. It was shocking, impossible, as if a friend had been killed, and it seemed at the time like the end of an era — I think it was in a way.

# 10

I had decided to rent the little flat in Battersea when Margaret, the girlfriend whose place I shared in Chelsea, went off travelling in Iran. Now I was on my own, free, for the first time, and I decorated my sitting room in shocking pink and orange — not very Little Grey Rabbit, but it was to match a rug I bought in a sale in a shop called Casa Pupo. Actually I wasn't entirely on my own because I shared the flat with an abandoned budgerigar that Mr Mead, the porter, gave me. I called the bird Jeremiah and let it fly around the kitchen until one day it escaped; I said a sad mental goodbye to him, but, astonishingly, a few days later a budgie turned up tapping at someone else's window in our block. Mr Mead heard about this and we went, armed with the cage, and sure enough it was Jeremiah who flapped straight in without a backward glance at liberty — you could almost hear his little bird brain going PHEW!

Mr Mead loved breaking bad news. He hovered on the pavement all day, ready to intercept passers-by, and his opening words were always: 'An 'orrible thing 'appened 'ere last night/this morning/yesterday.' In those days Battersea had not yet been gentrified, so horrible things happened quite often; my neighbour was stabbed (not fatally) when he asked a man not to pee on the landing outside our flats.

180

One day, as I came out on my way to work, Mr Mead cornered me and said: 'An 'orrible thing 'appened 'ere this morning: they stole Mrs Brown's TV set; can you believe it, they walked in bold as brass, went upstairs, picked the lock and walked out with it, just like those two blokes there' — we both looked at two men carrying a big television set across the pavement. 'How awful,' I responded and started walking towards the bus stop only to be stopped in my tracks a moment or so later by Mr Mead's shouts — the TV we'd just watched being carried out of the block was *his*.

★  ★  ★

Moira lived in a flat further up Prince of Wales Drive and we went to work together in my Mini Van. I have always been bad in the mornings and was usually running late, and as we batted along the South Bank, past Big Ben across the river, Moira used to joke, 'I hope to God that clock's fast.' Mrs Carter once said to me, 'Some people are paid for their time, and some for their talent, and in your case, dearie, I must assume it is the latter.' She used to ring me in the mornings at about eight when I was still fast asleep and say, 'Did I wake you, dear girl?' 'No! No!' I'd practically shout in my most hectically energetic voice. 'I've been up for hours.' I still answer the phone in that voice early in the morning, just in case.

One of the good things about being partly responsible for Mrs Carter's pictures was that she had to take me to Paris for the collections so that I could organise them there too. On second thoughts, I must be looking back through rose-tinted glasses because being in charge of photographing the Paris collections was frantic and stressful and incredibly hard work, and not much fun at all, except in retrospect. And getting there and back took so much time because I was terrified of flying, so used to travel on the overnight boat train from Victoria to the Gare du Nord.

During the collections, I was supposed to spend the days going to the fashion shows with Mrs Carter, which usually meant fighting my way into a place at the very back of a salon, or sitting on a radiator, or on the corner of someone else's chair, because, as a mere assistant, I had not been allocated anywhere to sit. (I'll always remember Gabrielle, the press officer at Yves Saint Laurent, who used to make sure I had a decent seat.) Being American, and chief fashion editor of an important paper, Mrs Carter herself was something of a celeb and would always have a place of honour in the front row, and just occasionally I would get to sit beside her and the rather camp American illustrator, Joe Eula, she always employed for the collections. I remember a Balmain show when Joe looked at the models with their bright-blue eyeshadow and pink cheeks and red lips, and whispered, '*Maquillage* by Walt Disney.' Once, Mrs Carter shocked everyone — including me — by leaving a Cardin show in the middle. Pierre Cardin's collections involved hundreds of garments and his shows dragged interminably, but this time Mrs Carter suddenly stood up and turned towards the exit. 'Madame Carter,' cried the *vendeuse* standing in the salon, '*Ce n'est pas finie.*' 'Well, it's *finie* as far as I am concerned,' said Mrs Carter firmly and continued on her journey.

Nowadays the Paris collections have become spectacles held in extraordinary venues, but in my day they took place in the actual showrooms of Dior or Chanel or Cardin or whoever, and I did once have the thrill of seeing Mademoiselle Chanel herself, reflected in mirrors, sitting on the staircase in her showroom in the Rue Cambon watching her own collection (exactly as she appears at the end of the film *Coco Before Chanel*).

We assistants were not invited to the glamorous parties that took place during Paris Fashion Week, but once in a blue moon Mrs Carter would take me with her — at one reception she asked me if I would like to meet her friend Gregory Peck and of course the answer was YES, but as I followed her through the densely crowded room someone squashed a chocolate éclair on my bosom (I was in a pale-blue silk suit) so I dropped out. A decade later, though, I was interviewing his French wife, Veronique, at the Savoy Hotel in London, when 'Greg', as she called him, came back early, and not only did I meet him, but he invited AW and me to stay with them in France — we were too overwhelmed to go. Veronique had been a journalist in Paris and they met when she was sent by her paper to interview him. They got on well, and next day he telephoned her — she was out, and a fellow journalist answered his call and left a message on her typewriter saying 'Gregory Peck called.' She thought it was a joke.

As she viewed the collections, Mrs Carter would note down the outfits she wanted photographed for her pages, and then, at night (we had to work at night because the clothes were shown to buyers during the day), I and whoever was Mrs Carter's junior assistant at the time (they changed quite frequently) would go and collect the outfits from Dior or Saint Laurent or whoever, take them to be photographed in the studio we had hired for the week, and then return them. Of course all the fashion editors would choose the same star outfits, so you had to hang around for hours in the middle of the night, waiting for *Vogue* or *Harper's* or the *Telegraph* to bring back the garment you wanted so that you could rush it to the studio. The worst thing that could happen was if Mrs Carter chose a dress or suit that had been shown on Hiroko, Pierre Cardin's star Japanese model, because she was so tiny that no one else could fit into her clothes, which meant you would have to go and collect Hiroko herself from her apartment and take her to the studio, as well as fetching her outfit from Cardin. Writing this, I can't believe the hassle we went through; but rushing round Paris in the middle of the night with armfuls of clothes, or getting food and drinks for everyone in the studio at three in the morning, wasn't always the worst of it — you could hit an unexpected problem: my very dear friend the photographer Terence Donovan, who was going through some personal difficulties at the time, announced that he couldn't photograph anything unless he could listen to Churchill's wartime speeches. I can't remember how, but we actually managed to get the recorded speeches (it was through the British Embassy in Paris in some way) and a *Sunday Times* colleague went off and bought a gramophone and lugged it to the studio, and we got the collections photographed. (Astonishing to think that now the speeches could have simply been downloaded from a mobile phone.)

My most stressful Paris collections experience was after the launch of the *Sunday Times* colour magazine in 1962; but I'll come back to that in a moment.

⋆ ⋆ ⋆

Giving readers a free magazine with their Sunday newspaper was an American idea which our editor, Denis Hamilton, was the first to introduce in Britain — it was such an innovation that to start with they called it the *Sunday Times Supplement* so as not to scare 'real' magazine producers. When it came to designing the launch cover, it was decided by Michael Rand, the art director, that it should feature the things that represented the country at its best — British icons, if you like — and I was asked to book Bailey to do photographs of Jean Shrimpton in something representing the new youthful British fashions. I chose a Mary Quant dress in grey flannel and we went down to the Thames by Lots Road Power Station to do the pictures; it was freezing cold. Later, when he laid out the cover, Michael Rand added a picture of a footballer — and that was the one-page portrait of Britain in 1962: football, Bailey, Jean and Mary Quant. Like 'Autumn Girl', this became *Bailey's* picture — no one ever mentions that I was involved at all, but I guess that's life; anyway, I am mentioning it now.

When the time came for the magazine's first coverage of the Paris collections, I talked Mrs Carter (who was now fashion editor of both newspaper *and* magazine) into taking Bailey and Jean to Paris to do the pictures because I was so at ease and happy working with both of them by then. Mrs Carter needed persuading because she hadn't, at the start, at all approved of the takeover of the fashion world by youngsters: she had refused to look at Mary Quant's clothes, for instance, but now she was just beginning to come round to the idea (she later considered Mary as important a fashion designer as Chanel and Dior). Her conversion was partly because the American press, particularly the powerful (and terrifying) Diana Vreeland of *Vogue*, who is said to have coined the word 'Youthquake' for what was going on in London, loved it all so much. (That season in Paris — or it might have been the next one — I saw Mrs Vreeland kiss David Bailey's hand at a party and I knew that he would fly so high that I would probably not be doing the Paris collections with him for very much longer.)

Bailey and Jean and I went to Paris with Mrs Carter; this was the very first time he had covered the Paris collections, and it got off on a bad footing when his camera broke and we had to borrow another one from a charming Australian photographer called Alec Murray. He lent Bailey one of his without a quibble, which was pretty decent in view of the fact that young snappers like Bailey were shortly to put the old ones like Alec out of work.

For some obscure reason, Mrs Carter wanted the pictures done in the gardens at Versailles, which meant me keeping the clothes that were to be photographed in my hotel room overnight so we could set off at first light. One of the dresses she'd chosen was a long evening gown from Nina Ricci; it was called 'Ondine' and was made of yards and yards of pleated pale-green chiffon. I remember it only too well — it is engraved on my soul actually — because I tried the dress on in my hotel room that evening (what girl wouldn't have?), stood on the bed to get a better view in the mirror, lost my balance and fell, putting my foot through the hem and ripping a huge hole. I sat up half the night sewing it up with dozens of little hotel mending kits I got from the concierge. When I returned the dress next day my heart was pounding — I had visions of them charging me thousands of pounds, but no one noticed the tear.

At Versailles it was bitterly cold (it was January) and Jean — who had to change in the open air — was freezing to death, but she and

Bailey just got on with it and the pictures were great (they were in black and white so you couldn't see that Jean was blue). When I think of Linda Evangelista's famous comment about not getting out of bed for less than ten thousand dollars a day, or read about Naomi Campbell's tantrums, I think back to that morning at Versailles and realise how lucky I was to have worked in fashion at a time when everyone was a friend, and we were all excited amateurs, learning on the job, trying our best to get our ideas across — and fashion had not yet become corporate Big Business.

I had other reasons to be grateful to Bailey and Jean: they often helped out if I needed an urgent picture taken. Not long after we'd all come back from Paris, I had a dozen outfits to get photographed for the *Sunday Times* colour magazine. The photographer I'd chosen went on an alcoholic binge and, though I had booked him and the model for *two days*, he didn't manage to take a single picture.

I was panicking — by now it was Friday evening, I had nothing to give the magazine, and the deadline was Monday morning. I rang Bailey and implored him to photograph the clothes on Jean over the weekend (they lived together at the time). He said he'd try if I ferried them over to his house. On the Monday morning he told me that they hadn't managed to get around to doing the pictures, but it was a typical Bailey joke — the transparencies were on their way in a taxi.

★ ★ ★

At around this time, a model I was working with changed my life. She was Nicole de Lamargé, the girlfriend (and favourite model of the day) of the photographer and art director Peter Knapp, who, together with its dynamic founder and editor Hélène Gordon-Lazareff, had made the French *Elle* magazine the most sought-after across the globe. Nicole had come from Paris to work in London for a spell; she was the most professional model girl in the world, a master of make-up who could transform her face in a dozen different ways; she invented cheek-shading and highlighting to give 'good bones' as well as painted-on freckles and eyelashes (ages before Twiggy); and she always posed with a full-length mirror in front of her so that she could see exactly how to 'work' the clothes she was wearing. I had booked Norman Eales to do my photographs that day; I loved working with him — like John French in the Fifties, he knew how to create real *glamour* in his pictures, and I have never understood why he is not on the list when people talk about the great Sixties photographers David Bailey, Brian Duffy and Terence Donovan; perhaps it was because, being gay, he didn't fit the macho, laddish narrative the newspapers had created about them, or maybe it was because he worked mostly for *Cosmopolitan* magazine and not *Vogue*. (Before it came out in 1972 I was interviewed, among many others I suspect, for the post of editing the British edition of *Cosmopolitan* by Helen Gurley Brown — famous for her book *Sex and the Single Girl* and for turning American *Cosmo* into a spectacularly

189

successful magazine. She asked me whether, as editor, I would be thinking of the magazine *every minute of every hour of every day* . . . She might have noticed my hesitation before I said, 'Yes of course,' because I didn't get the job.)

Anyway, Nicole and I were, quite unusually, waiting in the dressing room at *Vogue* studios for Norman to turn up, when she suddenly asked if she could do my make-up. I'd come out of my Beatnik phase by then, and can't remember now what kind of half-hearted job I did with lipstick and eyeshadow, pre-Nicole — but that morning, she transformed my face from completely nondescript into something quite glamorous by painting on rather extreme eye make-up involving white highlights and grey shadow and black pencil and drawn-on false eyelashes. 'Baboon eyes', my aunt called them when she first saw my new look, but I loved this version of myself and from that moment I never went out without my eye make-up, even though it took ages to put on.

Back at the newspaper, after much scheming and plotting between me and Meriel, my dear friend from the *Daily Express*, Mrs Carter hired Meriel as her new assistant. 'What is your star sign, dearie?' asked Mrs Carter the first day she arrived for work. 'Libra,' said Meriel. 'Oh dear,' said Mrs C, 'I am Libra too, I am afraid we will not get on.' She was right — they were a disastrous combination — but it ended up happily, with Meriel becoming a brilliant fashion editor of the colour magazine, while Mrs Carter and I stayed in charge of fashion on the main paper.

For me, one of the best things about Meriel coming to the *Sunday Times* was that we got to work at the Paris collections together. In January 1964 (before Meriel moved over to the magazine) we were told by Mrs Carter to cover an opening show by a more or less unknown designer André Courrèges; she herself couldn't be there for some reason. We went along — and became part of fashion history: it was a spectacular, innovative collection in which Courrèges showed beautiful, simple clothes in pale gaberdine fabric, with skirts *above the knee*, worn with short flat white boots. It shook fashion like an 8.0 earthquake. I don't think Mrs Carter believed us when we reported on the collection — especially the short skirts — but she soon had to, because the tremors were being felt everywhere. Jean Shrimpton wore a short skirt to the Melbourne Races the following year and made banner headlines — there couldn't have been more fuss if she'd gone topless, though when you look at the photographs now, the skirt length seems positively demure. There has always been controversy about who invented the miniskirt — was it Mary Quant or Courrèges, or even John Bates? My answer would be Courrèges — because I saw the skirts at that collection with my own eyes, and they were well above the knee, and I'd never come across anything like them before in London.

I missed Meriel when she finally went off to the magazine, but if she hadn't gone to work in colour, my favourite story about her would never

191

have happened — I have heard various versions as it gets repeated over and over again, but this is the true one, straight from the horse's mouth. Meriel went on a fashion shoot to Goa with the Dutch photographer Sacha, her partner and a model girl. One afternoon they came across a shop selling the most wonderful clothes — Indian-style tunics and trousers in pale faded cottons. They were wildly excited and started pulling the outfits off the shelves, and then Meriel said, 'We must be organised about this: we'll make a pile of the things we like, and then we'll find out how much they cost.' At which point the owner of the establishment said, 'Oh, madame, I am so sorry but this is not a shop, it is a laundry.'

# 11

People always put the Sixties and illicit drugs together (if you can remember the Sixties you weren't really there etc.), but in the early years of the decade no one took drugs, except speed, which we thought was a slimming tablet. I interviewed Mary Quant about twenty years after her heyday and in the course of the conversation asked whether she'd taken drugs. She frowned at me as though I was being silly: 'Of course not,' she said.

I do remember Harold Carlton, an artist friend who lived in New York, coming back to London and telling me about LSD. Should I try it? I wondered, and Harold said, 'It's up to you, I will give you a sugar lump with LSD on it and you can decide.' He gave me the lump and I put it in my sugar bowl while I thought about it. In fact, I more or less forgot about it until a couple of days later when, in the office, I remembered that my cleaning lady was due in my flat that morning, and she took sugar in her tea and PERHAPS SHE WOULD PUT THE LSD IN HER TEA AND GO CRAZY. I rang Harold hysterically, and he told me there was no LSD on the sugar lump — 'I would never have done that to you,' he said. (I later discovered that this cleaning lady had, over time, stolen nearly all the beautiful clothes I had acquired, at wholesale prices, as a fashion editor, so I rather wished that the sugar lump had been laced with a triple dose of LSD, and that she *had* taken it.)

Harold Carlton invented the graphic letter in which, instead of writing in the normal way, you stuck pictures taken in a photo-booth on to the paper and wrote witty captions for them. I persuaded my assistant, Edwina, to come with me to Woolworths in Holborn to help me with a return photo-letter to Harold. We took a bag of accessories and were in the booth for a long time, dressing up, putting on hats and make-up for the different pictures, when suddenly, under the curtain, a man exposed himself. We cowered in the corner, cringing as far from the horrible sight as we could — we worried it might be in the picture, in which case Harold would think we'd gone too far — and then I plucked up the courage and pulled the curtain back and told the exposer to go away. He was a weedy little bloke and ran off looking scared.

It wasn't illegal substances in the early Sixties, but cigarettes and alcohol that we consumed in large quantities. Everyone smoked everywhere — in theatres and cinemas and planes and through meals: there was some public debate about whether it was bad manners to smoke between courses, but we were smoking between *mouthfuls*; the cigarettes would be smouldering away in ashtrays next to our plates as we alternated a forkful of food with a puff on the fag.

Alcohol was responsible for most of the stupid scrapes I got into. To my embarrassment, even as I write this, one of them involved Gerald Scarfe, the great cartoonist. The story started in France. Meriel and Michael Rand, the art director of the colour magazine, were always thinking up new ways of covering the Paris collections, and one year Gerald Scarfe was invited to *draw* the shows, particularly the audiences of celebs and important fashion editors: Eugenia Sheppard of the *Herald Tribune*, Diana Vreeland of American *Vogue*, Beatrix Miller of British *Vogue*, Winefride Jackson of the *Telegraph*, Iris Ashley of the *Daily Mail*, etc.

We stayed together in the Hôtel de La Trémoille — Meriel and I always stayed there for the Paris collections; in fact we got to know it so well that when, later on, the hotelier Charles Forte took over the establishment and refurbished it, we bought the old brass beds that had been in our rooms. Anyway, at some stage during this visit Gerald mentioned that he never liked to see his cartoons framed as they were not meant to be 'art' but commentary.

More than a year after this, Meriel and I and Derek, my boyfriend of the time, happened to be invited to dinner by friends who were renting an apartment in Gerald's house, and in the stairwell there were some of his cartoons, *framed*. By the end of the evening, we had all had far too much to drink and, giggling like fools, we decided that Derek and I should steal all the pictures. With our friends' help we unhooked them from the walls and loaded them into my Mini and drove home (no drink-driving rules in those days) across the river to my flat in Battersea.

Next morning it was the Wake of Shame as,

through my dreadful hangover, I remembered the crime I had committed. I was still in the flat, desperately late for work, wondering what on earth to do, when Meriel rang from the *Sunday Times* office, where Gerald was employed at that time. 'He is furious,' she whispered, 'but says he will take no action if you return the pictures.' I drove my Mini back to Chelsea Embankment, parked at the end of the path to his house, and then carried in the cartoons — it took more than one journey — until they were all stacked by his front door. I have never felt so foolish, especially as I imagined he was probably watching from a window.

# 12

In 1965 the hairdresser Vidal Sassoon opened his first salon outside England, on Madison Avenue in New York. By now he was famous — apart from anything else, he cut Mary Quant's hair and she was even more famous, iconic even — so this opening, which was to be celebrated with a glittering party, was a major event in the fashion world, and the *Sunday Times* sent me to cover the story. It cost the newspaper a fortune, I discovered after I came home, because I couldn't decide which celebrity photo to wire to London with my story, so, being completely ignorant of the procedure, I sent them four or five. 'You could have bought a little car with what that cost,' one of the printers told me later.

\* \* \*

I don't know if all my generation of women were painfully shy and inept at handling predatory men, but I certainly was, and I seemed to give out such a feeble, 'no threat' vibe that I was always being flashed at or followed on the tube. My worst experience — and it's painful to think it was my own fault — took place on that same visit to New York. A good friend (she was another English journalist there to write about Vidal Sassoon's new salon) asked me to make up a four for an evening at El Morocco, the most famous nightclub in New York; I would be a blind date for her American boyfriend's mate, an older man.

At the end of the evening my 'date' said he would take me home, but instead, a chauffeur drove us to his apartment, where he asked me up for a coffee. I definitely didn't want to go, and asked if the chauffeur couldn't just take me home, but the chauffeur said it wasn't his business, and the 'date' convinced me that there was no hidden agenda and I felt rude to refuse — we were all so ridiculously polite and naive in those days — so I went up with him and as soon as he'd closed the door of his apartment he jumped on me. I fought him furiously, and managed to get away, but in the course of the struggle he ripped my dress all down the back, and now I had to walk through the streets of New York at two in the morning to where I was staying with another English girlfriend, and my clothes were falling off me, and my hair was standing on end, and of course I had no phone. I remember being petrified that I'd be attacked again, and so thankful that New York was designed on a grid pattern so I couldn't get lost.

\* \* \*

My sister Tessa had gone to work in Hong Kong, and I missed her so much that I saved up and went to visit her in my holidays — and there I was struck by what I thought was a terrific moneymaking idea. That year, 1966, Yves Saint Laurent had shown a series of spectacular, boldly striped dresses, just like knee-length T-shirts but entirely covered with sequins — no one had seen anything like them before. (It was an expensive copy of one of these that Norman Eales had photographed for me on Shirley Fossett, the trapeze artist.) Now, in Hong Kong, I could tell that it would probably not be too difficult to make much cheaper versions of these dresses out there. I knew absolutely nothing about how to set about doing this and in any case I had to go home, so I left it all in Tessa's hands, and after a couple of false trails, she managed to find someone who could copy the dresses, and they produced a handful of samples that I showed to Meriel when they arrived. Meriel thought they were stunning and decided to photograph them for the colour mag; she interviewed me about how they came into being and, without much consideration, I related Tessa's difficulties finding a manufacturer — mentioning that at one stage a Chinese businessman had taken her in a Rolls-Royce to look at a factory that turned out not to belong to him. (Tessa had told me she'd gone in a very expensive car, but I didn't know what it was . . . I just said Rolls-Royce because it was the most costly motor I could think of.)

Meriel's story appeared in the magazine and, next thing, the Hong Kong Government was suing the *Sunday Times* for damaging the island's manufacturing reputation. The only Rolls-Royce there, it turned out, belonged to the Governor. I had to go to Harry Evans, the editor at the time, and confess that I had lied about the car. Somehow he smoothed it all over, and that was the last I heard of it, but it kept me awake at night for months.

In Hong Kong, Tessa and I met a charming Chinese man Albert Poon; he had nothing to do with our efforts to make sequined dresses, but was keen to open a London-style boutique in Hong Kong — it would be a first for the island. Albert's father, a judge, had sent him to sixth form at Millfield in Somerset where, he told us, sixth-form boys were allowed to smoke, but just *pipes*; only sixth-form girls could smoke cigarettes. Albert was hilarious about his own Chinese/English culture clashes. Some time after he left school the new posh friends he'd made there invited him to go shooting and, not knowing the protocol for such an outing, Albert had accepted the invitation and turned up with something like a machinegun — they were appalled. 'Poon,' they cried, 'for God's sake put that in the car where no one can see it, and borrow a proper gun.' Since I was viewing all the dress collections in London anyway, Albert wondered if I could order the clothes for his boutique and, in exchange, he would give me a return air ticket to Hong Kong so I could visit Tessa. It sounded to me like a great idea.

When Trend Gallery (as it was called) eventually opened, Albert celebrated by taking us all out to supper in Hong Kong; my soup had a cockerel's head floating in it and Michael Shea, the shop manager, whispered to me that, according to Chinese custom, I had to eat it or it would be an insult to our host. I sat there, almost in tears, knowing that I would *have* to be rude to Albert, because I couldn't even look at it, let alone touch it, let alone SWALLOW it. The guests sat, stony-faced, watching me for what seemed like an age, but all of a sudden they burst into laughter and it turned out to be a joke.

Trend Gallery was beautifully fitted out, and very central, but it never became quite as successful as it should have, because though it was aimed at Westerners, the manager and the chief shop assistant were Chinese and so the customers it attracted tended to be Chinese too — very quickly, we had to start ordering clothes in sizes 6 and 8 instead of 12 and 14.

Then Albert branched out into hair. The Cultural Revolution had just started in China, and Chinese women had to cut their hair short, meaning that there were literally tons and tons of the stuff coming on to the market. This coincided with a sudden craze for wigs and hairpieces in the Western world — or perhaps it wasn't a coincidence, perhaps the glut of hair led to the passion for hairpieces. Somehow I was talked into trying to sell Albert's hair in London and, goodness knows how, I found a man who had a concession at one of the big supermarket chains, who ordered a few dozen of a straight, shoulder-length bob stitched to an Alice band. The trouble was that when the package arrived in London, the hair wasn't straight, but frizzy, and Moira and I had to stay up late for nights on end, ironing it. I can't really believe I am writing this; sometimes now my younger self astonishes me.

I also ordered a whole lot of little ringlets on kirby grips which you were supposed to push into your hair above your ears to give a sort of wispy Twiggy look. These did arrive as per the specification, but unfortunately at that moment the bloke with the concession went bust and never took the ringlets, which were still in a box under my bed almost a decade later, long after I had met and married AW and had children. He suggested that if we stitched them to homburg hats we might find a market among bald members of the Hasidic sect of Jews who are not allowed to cut their sideburns.

In the event, I don't know what happened to the ringlets; AW probably threw them out when I wasn't looking.

All in all, my business ventures in Hong Kong were about as successful as my mouse-skin fur coats in Somerset; but even though none of them worked, it had all been extraordinary and exciting — I still keep a sequin dress in the attic in case I ever wonder if I made the whole thing up.

# 13

In the early Sixties our forward-looking editor, Denis Hamilton, who had just launched the *Sunday Times* colour magazine, started a new investigative column called 'Insight' which later became famous for its coverage of the thalidomide disaster and led to the victims of the drug being properly compensated.

'Insight' recruited feisty young Australian journalists, and a whole gang of these suddenly invaded the paper — the most colourful of them, Murray Sayle, becoming a legendary correspondent. In the course of his career with the paper Murray climbed Mount Everest (he didn't get to the top), sailed across the Atlantic single-handed, tracked down Che Guevara in the Bolivian jungle and the spy Kim Philby in Moscow. But Murray's greatest renown in the newspaper world was for his wildly inventive expenses claims. Once, on a sailing story, he put down a claim for 'old rope' and got it — money for old rope. It was probably the very least amount he fiddled, but everyone loved the wit.

The now-famous war photographer Don McCullin joined the paper at around the same time, and all of a sudden the *Sunday Times* had perhaps the best and bravest group of reporters ever to work together on a publication. There was a new macho mood that could be felt even in the offices of the Women's Pages (for a start, we were all in love with Don who was extremely handsome striding about in his battle-worn fatigues — at least that's what we liked to think they were — but also disarmingly modest. He once gave me an old *Girl's Own Annual*; I was the envy of my colleagues and I still have it).

I became friendly with two of the young Aussies, Tony Clifton and Alex Mitchell, who were irreverent and funny and on a mission to make the world better; they nicknamed me Battersea Bridge because of where I lived. I admired them greatly and, largely because of them, spent my weekends on protest marches. There were so many demonstrations and protests in the Sixties — I remember a bewildered policeman trying to sort out a muddle of marchers in Trafalgar Square, yelling: 'Civil rights for Ireland over to the right please, Biafra to the left, CND wait over there, Vietnam down the middle.' There was no kettling of protesters in those days.

The young Aussies, who were Marxists, made me feel a bit of a wimp being on the Women's Pages; they'd say, 'Aw, come on, Bridge, do you seriously want to spend the rest of your life in *fashion?*', and they fired me up to do something more daring and serious — such as go to Vietnam and try to be a war reporter.

In 1967 I was leaving the *Sunday Times* anyway because I'd been recruited as assistant editor of a brand-new magazine — *Élan*, it was called — so I decided to take a bit of time off between jobs and go to the Far East where I could a) check up on Tessa who had moved from

Hong Kong to Bangkok (Mum was worried about her being away so long, and wanted me to try and persuade her to come home), b) visit Hong Kong and see Albert Poon and all my friends connected with the shop and the hair, and c) stop off in Vietnam and become a world-famous war correspondent. (The *Sunday Times* news editor agreed that if I came up with any stories he would give them due consideration.) And d) Tessa and I could visit our cousin Simon (now a British Army officer), temporarily serving with the Trucial Scouts in Dubai.

Extraordinarily, the other day, in a box in the attic, I found the bill for my ticket for this journey; it says London — Bangkok — Saigon — Hong Kong — New Delhi — Bombay — Dubai — London, £395.

Just before I left the paper I did perhaps my starriest fashion piece — on the Beatles' wives; well, three wives and a sister-in-law: Maureen Starr (Ringo's wife), Cynthia Lennon (John's wife), Pattie Harrison (George's wife) and her sister Jenny, because Paul didn't have a wife then. The photograph was taken by Ronald Traeger and it came out in the paper in September 1967. I think the wives agreed to do the story because they were eager to promote their new discovery: a group of Dutch hippy designers — they called themselves The Fool — whose crazy clothes they loved and wore themselves, and had chosen to stock in the Beatles' new boutique, Apple, which was about to open in Baker Street. We all met up at the studio and I was amazed how pleasant and unspoiled they seemed to be; I don't remember any security people being there, and I don't think we even had a hairdresser. I felt a bit sorry for Cynthia Lennon because, though the others all had the same Sixties look with pretty elfin faces almost hidden by their long hair and fringes, she was in a different mould — a bit plumper (which is why I think we put her at the back) and round-faced, and I had to spend some time trying to get her curlier, shorter hair to look the same as everyone else in the picture.

# 14

Before I set out on my great Eastern adventure, Tessa decided that she *would* like to come home with me at the end of the trip, and in the meantime she would join me on my travels, and so we met in Bangkok and flew together from there to Tan Son Nhut (as it was then known) airport in Vietnam.

On the plane we had to fill in our Vietnamese immigration forms — I put '*Sunday Times* reporter' (later I was awarded a press card by the Vietnamese authorities as well as one from the US Army, giving me the title of honorary major), but Tessa put 'Tourist', which meant that every morning in our hotel we were telephoned by the Minister of Tourism *himself* offering us an excursion to Dalat, a beautiful place in the mountains. We were keen to go, and he agreed to take us, but in the meantime there was always the small problem that the Vietcong had seized the road in the night and we would just have to wait through the day until the Americans got it back again; he'd let us know. We never did get to Dalat, but the Tourist Office sent round some brochures for Tessa: one of them said 'Go for a walk in the fairytale woods that surround Saigon.'

Tan Son Nhut was the busiest airport in the world at that time, and Tessa and I hadn't given a single thought as to how quickly we would be able to get a flight out of Vietnam and on to Hong Kong, so, though we'd planned to be there for five or six days, we ended up having to spend more than three weeks in Saigon (now Ho Chi Minh City) before we could get seats on a plane.

Neither had we given a thought to what a war reporter should *wear* — we just went in our normal London clothes. I clearly remember the look of incredulity, mixed with horror, mixed with thin humour, that crossed the face of the *Sunday Times*'s Far East correspondent, David Bonavia (who had been asked to meet us at the airport), when he saw us coming through Customs towards him in our miniskirts. He took us to the 'journalists' hotel' in Saigon, the Caravelle, which had a pavement café/bar with wire netting around it so that grenades couldn't be chucked in, and introduced us to some reporters and then, probably with a sigh of relief, he rather disappeared out of our lives.

The journalists — some British, some Australian, some American — were welcoming, suggesting stories I might do, and generally trying to be helpful. A few of them have remained friends to this day, and one of them, Derek, an Aussie, came into my life in a serious way after I got back to London; we went out together for two years — he was my accomplice when we stole Gerald Scarfe's pictures. We went to France together on holiday which was very daring in those days, and the hotel receptionist gave him the registration form to fill in. 'Hey,' he said, 'the French are so open-minded, there is even a place on this form to put the name of the girl you're with,' and he pointed to where it said *Nom de Jeune Fille*. Sadly, I pointed out that this meant Maiden Name, and not Name of Your Young Girlfriend, in French. He was very disappointed. Mum and Dad didn't like him at all — once we turned into their driveway and we could hear, quite clearly through the open windows, Dad calling out: 'Here's Brigid with that awful man again.' (This was quite unusual for Dad whose normal comment on meeting our boyfriends was: 'Well, he'll be bald by the time he's thirty.')

★ ★ ★

Back in the Caravelle café in Saigon, it turned out that *I* might be able to help the journalists — there had recently been an election in Vietnam and the new president, an army officer, Nguyen Van Thieu, was being difficult with the press corps about interviews. But our new friends thought he might agree to see me, a woman and a fresh face on the scene, so they offered to write my questions and lend me a tape recorder if I would share the results with them. Amazingly enough, they were right, I *did* get an interview with President Thieu — I was all set for my SCOOP, but the day before my appointment, something happened to my throat, I couldn't speak, and Tessa had to cancel it. I had no idea what was wrong: I had a huge lump in my throat and watering eyes and I had to keep swallowing — with great difficulty — every five seconds; at the time I thought I must have got

209

cancer, but now I know it was my voice having a nervous breakdown at the very idea of interviewing the President of Vietnam with an unfamiliar tape recorder, and a list of political questions about a war and a country I knew very little about. It took a week or more for my voice to start going back to normal.

★   ★   ★

Saigon was an attractive city that could almost have been in France, with its outdoor cafés, and people on bikes and scooters; but there were coolie hats and policemen in khaki shorts with thin brown legs, and slender black-haired Vietnamese women in traditional, skin-tight *ao dai* dresses to remind us that we were in the Orient, and most of all there was a perpetual THUD THUD THUD in the air from endless helicopters flying over the place, and a pit of fear in our stomachs to remind us that we were in a war zone. Not long before we arrived, a woman they called the Dragon Lady had been scaring Saigon: she would appear from nowhere, riding on the back of a motorbike, and open fire on US soldiers on the streets.

I had booked us into the Majestic Hotel which overlooked the Saigon River; I think our room was on the third floor, but every time we got into the elevator, the lift boy would press the button for the top floor where there was a popular bar. The doors would open, the crowd of American soldiers would turn to see who was coming in, and there were Tessa and I in miniskirts, the only two 'round eyes' in town apart from the *real* women war correspondents (a couple of whom had been banned from going to US bases because their toughness demoralised the troops who preferred to think of 'their' Western women as gentle and soft-spoken). There would be yelps and shrieks of delight, while we would be frantically wrestling with the lift boy, trying to press all the buttons for any other floor, just to get us out of there.

As we kept writing to Mum, who was desperately worried about us, we were in the *centre* of Saigon and did not feel in any danger from the enemy — little knowing that the Tet Offensive, when waves of Vietcong fighters came right into the heart of the city, was to happen shortly after we left. Instead, as we did NOT report to Mum, we did feel wary of the US Army. I am not saying this in a vain way — we could have been the two Ugly Sisters, we could actually have been Cro-Magnons or Neanderthals: just being female and Western and in our twenties made us horribly desirable to the American soldiers, even after we'd swapped the miniskirts for trousers.

We were adopted by an American officer who'd taken a shine to Tessa — I think we met him at one of the evening press briefings (which, in my role as 'war correspondent', I solemnly insisted we attend) — and this was quite a good thing in the way that when you are surrounded by a gang of beggars in Morocco or India, it is better to select one as your 'guide', and then the others will leave you alone. But I never quit

211

Tessa's side for an instant. One afternoon the officer invited us back to his army quarters in Saigon to buy something in the PX (the store for military personnel), or for tea, I don't remember. Time went by, and then, suddenly, it was: 'Whoops! Oh dear! I am so sorry, but I can't take you back to your hotel now because the curfew has started, and we would be shot.'

We had to stay in his room which had two beds, one empty. (Why? Had he got his room-mate to move out? Was this all planned in advance?) Tessa and I slept in one bed and he in the other, and every time he turned over in the night I was awake and on the alert to protect Tessa, but he made no move. The worst part was that in the morning he had to drive us back to our hotel in his jeep in front of everyone. We decided that he had set the whole thing up just so that all his friends and other soldiers would see him with not one, but TWO young Western girls, who had obviously spent the night with him. It was deeply embarrassing, I wanted to call out: 'IT'S NOT WHAT YOU THINK. NOTHING HAPPENED AT ALL.' In fact, he was a kind-hearted man, with a wife and family he loved in the States, and I don't think he minded too much me supergluing myself to Tessa as her chaperone; in fact he was probably a bit relieved.

He arranged an extraordinary trip for us — to visit the Filipino base in Tây Ninh Province, stopping on the way at the famous Cao Dai temple. Before we left, Tessa asked him what we should wear — 'I guess you should go for something like these fatigues,' he replied, indicating his own khaki camouflage combat shirt and trousers. 'Oh they're very nice,' said Tessa. 'I wonder if they come in other colours?' She has never lived it down.

# 15

The journey to Tây Ninh was in a Huey military helicopter flying over hostile territory, mostly denuded of vegetation by Agent Orange. It was the most frightening trip I have ever made in my life; I think Tessa and I only agreed to it in the first place because of Dad's constant advice '*Il faut saisir les occasions . . .*' ringing in our ears. We had young armed machine-gunners on either side of the helicopter, strapped to ledges on the *outside*; a big open door; and a few seats inside. 'You know, a single shot from the ground could bring this chopper down,' said one of the gunners casually as we were climbing in, and my true nature as a total coward was revealed as I headed for the innermost seat, which meant that Tessa had to sit by the door.

The Cao Dai temple was almost worth the terror. Tây Ninh and the temple both come into Graham Greene's novel *The Quiet American*, but we hadn't read it then, and had never heard of Caodaism before; now we discovered that it was/is the religion of several million Vietnamese. It seemed a wonderfully open-hearted one, with Jesus, Buddha, Muhammad, Victor Hugo, Joan of Arc, Julius Caesar and Sun Yat-sen as saints, and the temple itself a delicious kitsch fantasy of blue pillars with red dragons twined around them, and stained-glass windows, and walls painted bright yellow with dashes of shocking pink and red here and there. Imagine the gaudiest Chinese decorations and multiply them by two and you have something approaching the Cao Dai temple.

Our visit to the Filipinos, which was next on the itinerary, happened to be on the same day as an official tour by one of the American ambassadors to Vietnam at the time (there were two). Tessa and I were put sitting next to him to watch a parade, and we both had the same thought — that when someone tried to assassinate him they would miss and hit us instead, so whenever he leaned towards us to say anything, we craned our heads as far away from him as our necks would bear; I expect he guessed why.

The Filipinos were almost as pleased to see us as the American troops in Saigon, and persuaded Tessa and me to be photographed pretending to load a mortar with bombs — we knew this wasn't really appropriate, but everyone had been so kind to us and we were polite girls, and it did seem rude to refuse, so there we are, immortalised in these pictures, posing with the shells in our hands, and smiling like two fools. If we'd known about the controversy that would be caused, five years later, by photographs of Jane Fonda sitting on an anti-aircraft gun on her visit to North Vietnam, we might have thought twice about it. But this was early days, the Vietnam War was not yet the target of universal disapproval — we had friends in London who even supported it; and by the time the great anti-Vietnam protests took place in 1968, I am happy to say we were onside.

\* \* \*

We were asked if we would visit wounded American soldiers who were being treated in an inflatable hospital nearby. These extraordinary places were made on the same principle as bouncy castles, but on a huge scale; the advantage of them was that a whole sterile hospital unit could be pumped up anywhere, at a moment's notice; the danger being that if it was hit, the inflatable hospital collapsed on top of the patients — which did indeed happen in Vietnam, though this applied to solid buildings too.

Most of the very young men we talked to were suffering from the same kind of injuries, caused by *punji* traps; these were carefully disguised pits in the ground lined with sharpened, poisoned bamboo staves (*punji* sticks, they were called). When patrolling soldiers stepped into one of these traps, the sticks would pierce through their boots and clothing and into their flesh, causing infections, and often meaning they had to have their feet or lower legs amputated. These were the young Americans we were asked to cheer up — their lives had been ruined, it was heartbreaking.

I had begun to realise, humbly, that I was not the stuff of war correspondents within about half a minute of our arrival — when I saw David Bonavia's face actually — and this was confirmed when Tessa had to cancel my scoop interview with President Thieu. I decided instead to do a story on women war correspondents (perhaps this was to atone for my own failure as one) so that at least I wouldn't return completely empty-handed, and now I concentrated on finding and interviewing some of them.

The Vietnam War was the first in which women reporters were authorised to go to the front line along with fighting soldiers — by the time Tessa and I were there, two women journalists had already been killed. Only one of the five women I spoke to had actually been *sent* to Vietnam; the others had come independently (rather like me but a million times more fearless) on the chance of being taken on by an agency or newspaper, and had succeeded — the Vietnam War was a great career opportunity for some. Cathy Leroy, who belonged to this group, was the most extraordinary member of the women's press corps: French and chic (she owned a Chanel suit in Paris), twenty-three years old, and tiny (five feet tall), she was the only reporter, man or woman, to have parachuted into action; she had also been kidnapped by the Vietcong and badly wounded in battle: five pounds of shrapnel had entered her body. I stood in awe of her, as did all the other correspondents, not to mention the American Army.

My story was illustrated with wonderful pictures of her and the other women reporters in action, taken by Nik Wheeler (one of the journalists we met on our first day who has remained a lifelong friend), and it appeared in *Nova* magazine a few months later.

Soon, our time in Saigon was coming to an

end because we had at last managed to find seats on a plane out, but Tessa and I had one last mission — to visit an English doctor friend-of-a-friend of our parents who was working in Cholon, the Chinese part of Saigon. We had been told about him and his good work in glowing terms and felt Mum and Dad would be pleased if we made the effort to see him. We never told them what happened during our visit.

He invited us to supper at his home, but I don't remember any food, only that he plied Tessa and me with wine, and then attempted, rather insistently, to snog us, under the pretext of showing us where to find the lavatory. We only discovered on the way home that he'd tried this on both of us.

What helped to bring the awkward evening to an end was me falling on to a huge brass tray on legs that served as a coffee table. To this day I don't quite know how it happened: I was just leaning over from the sofa to stub my cigarette out when my centre of gravity suddenly shifted and I toppled slowly forward, crashing on to the table which gave way under my weight so I ended up spread-eagled on the tray on the floor. It made such a noise and was so embarrassing that it was a good excuse to gather up our stuff and leave. After I became an ambassador's wife I sometimes used to torture myself imagining the same thing happening at some diplomatic function in Syria or India, where they go in for those brass-tray tables, and I would break into a cold sweat.

# 16

When we were in Vietnam we were told that if we heard an explosion, we should throw ourselves to the ground, covering our heads with our arms. Tessa and I once tried to do this in the smallest taxi in the world — a tiny French Simca in Saigon; it was a bit like two sardines trying to turn over in their tin. And then after we'd struggled to the floor, it transpired that the explosion we'd heard was nothing more than a car backfiring.

The effects of being in Vietnam, even though it was only for twenty-one days or so, lasted for ages; weeks after we were back in England we would throw ourselves to the ground at, literally, the drop of a hat — or if someone slammed a door or even put a cup back on a saucer noisily, which must have been a bit disconcerting for everyone around us. One of the women reporters I'd interviewed had said, 'Getting used to peace is the hard part,' but I never thought that could possibly apply to us.

⋆ ⋆ ⋆

We saw Albert Poon and our friends in Hong Kong, then stopped briefly in Thailand again (to collect Tessa's coat that she'd left behind) where we were invited to supper by a friend, Maeve Fort, who worked for the British Embassy in

Bangkok. It was a nerve-racking evening because as we arrived she told us that there was a cobra behind the fridge in her kitchen but she hadn't been able to get it out yet; I still had my horror of snakes and wondered how we'd cope if it emerged while we were there (it didn't). Then we paused for a day or two with friends in India — all this was free on our tickets — and finally began our homeward journey.

The highlight of this was to be a visit to our cousin Simon in Dubai, in the Trucial States (as the Emirates were known then), but as we checked in at the airport in Bombay they told us that we were not allowed to get off the plane in Dubai because we had no visa for that country.

OK, we said, we'll go on to London, but when we stopped in Dubai, which was a very small airport then, we decided to give it a go, so we crept off the plane and round to the door of the hold and got someone to unload our cases and then went and hid in a ladies' room until our plane had taken off again. It was the boldest thing we'd ever done and we were amazed that it had been so easy, but travelling *was* so much simpler then. It was even more so when my mother's friend Pauline flew from England to India on an Imperial Airways flight before the Second World War. One of their overnight stops — in those days planes didn't fly at night — was also in the Emirates, at Sharjah. Next day, when they were en route again, Pauline suddenly realised that she had left her handbag on the Customs counter there. It had her passport and all her documents inside, so, in desperation, she begged the steward to ask the pilot to turn back in order to collect it. The pilot agreed, they returned to Sharjah, and Pauline was reunited with her bag. That is a true story.

Now, in Dubai, hiding in the ladies' room, we were not worried; we knew that Simon would be waiting for us, and that he would be able to sort out our visa problem. But Simon had mistaken the time and was not there when we emerged from the ladies' and went through immigration, so Tessa and I were arrested and locked in a small room at the airport for what seemed like an awfully long time before he eventually arrived and got us out.

Dubai was like a dusty town in a cowboy film then, all one-storey houses — I went back there again for the first time forty years later, and couldn't believe it was the same place. Actually, on this second visit I thought it was PARADISE — mostly because it wasn't Kazakhstan where we were posted at the time. AW had arranged a weekend in Dubai together, as a treat. I was to break my journey back from a visit to England there, and he would fly down from Almaty to join me, and then we would both travel back to Kazakhstan together.

My plane arrived the night before AW's, so in the morning, on my way to breakfast, I went to the hotel receptionist, a charming Syrian, and explained that my husband would be coming in shortly and please could he tell him I was in the dining room. When AW arrived the receptionist said to him, 'Your rose is in the dining room.' Being an Englishman, AW didn't get this at all

— he stomped into the dining room and said, 'Hello darling, where is my rose?' 'What do you mean?' I asked. 'Well, the receptionist said, 'Your rose is in the dining room,' so where is it?' 'I think he meant me,' I said sadly. 'I think I am your rose.' AW looked seriously disappointed.

# 17

To Mum's relief, Tessa and I arrived safely back from our travels, and I went off to my new job at *Élan*, but while I'd been away, the owners (International Publishing Company) had decided not to launch a new title after all, and I was transferred to *Nova* magazine, which they also owned, to be assistant editor there. (I still have the dummy edition of *Élan*, the mag-that-never-was; perhaps it will be worth a fortune one day.)

This turned out to be another piece of luck: I think I was happier at *Nova* than in any other job. The magazine had being going for about two years by the time I arrived in 1968, and in those years the photographer Harri Peccinotti, who was art director; Molly Parkin, the fashion editor; and Dennis Hackett, the editor, had done some extraordinary, ground-breaking work. Dennis was full of ideas: he longed to publish *Nova* back to front because he noticed how people often read magazines backwards; or, for a piece on the Catholic sacrament of confession, he wanted to cut a hole in the page so the priest could be on one side of it and the penitent on the other — but his bosses always stopped these extravagances. *Nova* was daring, but not everyone approved — one of the first things I did there was a piece on brightly coloured underwear: tights, knickers, vests in vivid pinks, reds, purple, lime green, all wonderfully photographed in close-up (revealing no flesh), which earned me a severe letter of disapproval from an aunt.

For others, *Nova* was/is iconic: to this day when I tell people of a certain age that I worked there, they look at me with new respect — even reverence — and issues of 'vintage' *Novas* can now fetch eighty quid on eBay, not a bad return on 3s 6d or 4s a copy, which was what it cost.

I could never imagine why Dennis Hackett was on a women's magazine at all — he was a newspaperman, originally from Yorkshire, charismatic and plain-speaking — but he was the best editor ever. We all wanted to please him so we racked our brains for good ideas, and if he liked them he would back you to the hilt. He gave me such a wide brief: one moment I was interviewing Madame Binh, the Vietcong negotiator at the Paris peace talks in 1968, next I was in Rome spending a few days with the Italian socialite Princess Pignatelli who had just been nominated the Best-Dressed Woman in the World for the second time, in order to find out what went into achieving that title. (I discovered the princess was so dedicated to the cause that she even plucked the hairs out of her legs individually with tweezers.)

Dennis spent a fortune on another of our stories: 'What Paris could do for the Queen' (i.e., what the Queen would look like if she dressed in Paris). This was so complicated that it is difficult to explain here, but it involved finding out the Queen's vital statistics (I got them at Madame Tussauds); booking a model with the same measurements; commissioning André Courrèges, the Paris couturier, to design and make a suit for Her Majesty; and then photographing this on the model. In the meantime Carita, the leading cosmetics firm in Paris, and Alexandre, the world's top hairdresser then, redesigned her make-up and hair. After that, all the different images were sent off to some state-of-the-art retouching place in the US to be put on to a real photograph of the Queen — producing an (almost) authentic-looking picture of Queen Elizabeth as she would appear if her clothes and hair and make-up were done in Paris.

The only problem was that the retouching people in the States didn't understand that they should have lengthened the skirt of the suit (Courrèges, the pioneer of short skirts, had refused to make it any longer), so that when the pictures arrived at the British Customs and were opened, they showed the Queen in a miniskirt, and were confiscated. Dennis had to ask permission from the Palace to have them released.

The feature caused a big stir — it was bought by magazines all around the world — and it was reported back to Dennis that the Queen was quite amused by her revamped self: she thought we'd made her look like Queen Farah Diba of Iran.

Putting it all together took weeks, plus several trips to Paris, not to mention the costs — the suit, the photographs, the retouching — but it was enormous fun to do and added to *Nova*'s fame. It makes me sad to think that nowadays, with Photoshop, it could all have been achieved in about one and a half minutes.

Then Dennis sent me to India with *Nova's* star funny writer John Sandilands (sadly he died a few years ago) to do a story on the Nizam of Hyderabad, the richest of all the Indian princes. I was so scared of the flight that I booked an appointment with a hypnotist in Harley Street to see if he could help, but I never found out because when I got there he asked me to take off my bra and, as I couldn't really see what that had to do with fear of flying, I left.

For economy's sake, the Nizam story was to be combined with a couple of fashion shoots in Rajasthan, so we also had the photographer, Harri Peccinotti, and the gorgeous model Greta Norris with us (she became a lifelong friend). At one point during the fashion photography, Greta and I were shown around a princely palace in Rajasthan. We climbed all the way up to a viewpoint on some high turret and looked down into the courtyard below, where, to our horror, we could clearly see an elephant with five legs, one of them badly withered. 'Oh my God,' I said to Greta, 'look at that crippled elephant. Only in India would they keep an animal with a leg like that alive and not do something about it.' Full of concern, we both turned to our guide to see what he had to say — but he waggled his head and seemed embarrassed, and it suddenly dawned on us that we were not looking at a deformed elephant, but an elephant WITH AN ERECTION. I have never got over it.

In Hyderabad, John had a rather scary time — the Nizam demanded he wore a specially made military uniform and set him various challenges: e.g., to jump across a very deep and rather wide crevice in the hills near the city. One evening, in the dark, John was told to fill up a huge tin trunk with stones, which he and the Nizam (with help from the staff) then heaved on to the balcony above the palace swimming pool, and into the water. The object of all this was to make an enormous splash and give Greta, me and Princess Esra, the Nizam's wife, who were sitting chatting around the other end of the pool, the fright of our lives. It succeeded.

Harri Peccinotti did our fashion pictures in India, but another photographer, Greta's husband, Tony Norris, came out to do the Nizam story (he and Greta knew him already) and pictured the prince with his 200-piece solid-gold dinner service; in his 1916 custom-built yellow Rolls-Royce which had a crown on the top and a throne inside; and with boxes and boxes of stuff — crockery, toy trains, soap, tablecloths, linen, picture frames, furniture, you name it — that his grandfather (the richest man in the world) had bought from the Army and Navy Stores in Bombay.

Apparently, the old Nizam had paid a visit to the department store back in the Thirties, and its British manager had of course personally shown him round. At the end of the tour, the Nizam had not commented or bought a thing, so the manager said, 'Is there absolutely nothing in our shop that pleases you, Your Exalted Highness?' and the Nizam replied something along the lines of: 'You don't understand, I would like *everything* in the shop.' And so lorryloads of crates and packages were delivered to Hyderabad where they remained, mostly unopened, in one of the Nizam's many buildings.

We did more pictures in the grand old state palace, Falaknuma, a vast place which had a beautiful big silver mango tree in the hall with gold mangoes on it (I don't know what happened to the mango tree, but the building is now a luxury hotel run by the Taj group). Seeing all these treasures somehow infected John and me with greed — we went round the palaces praising everything: 'Oh, that's nice', 'That's REALLY pretty', 'That's beautiful', 'Look at that, it's gorgeous', vaguely hoping, I suppose, that the Nizam might give an object to us. We'd got into the habit of doing this, and one day John looked at a hideous life-size Victorian statue of a shepherdess and said, 'That's nice,' and the Nizam said, 'I'd like you to have it, John.' John was appalled but there was nothing he could do, and he had all the trouble and expense of getting it back to his home in England.

One evening the Nizam took us to a circus in Hyderabad. We sat in special seats — the rather rickety equivalent of the Royal Box — and at one stage the ringmaster tried to coax the biggest elephant to approach the Nizam and bow, but it all went wrong: the elephant came up nicely, and then turned round, slowly backed up to the

Nizam and did the most enormous poo. It reminded me of being taken to the circus in India when Tessa and I were small. Before the big-cats act began, they put up a kind of wobbly cage of bars around the circus ring, but just as the lions and tigers entered the arena, the cage fell down and most of the audience, including us, got up and ran.

John had a curious experience in Hyderabad: one day three of us went out to explore the dry scrubby land beyond the palace, and, as we walked along, John lobbed his empty cigarette lighter far into the bushes. We were not aware that anyone had followed, or was watching us, but that evening John found the lighter placed ostentatiously on the desk in his room. It was quite creepy.

★   ★   ★

Christmas was coming and I had promised my parents to get home in time to be with them, so when the Nizam invited us all to stay on and celebrate with him and Princess Esra, I had to refuse. He was upset because he was planning all kinds of fun, but I had to stick to my plan and not disappoint the family. A few days later he invited John, Tony and Greta to go into his jewel vault and choose a Christmas present (they chose diamond watches); I was not included because I was not going to be there on Christmas Day. Then, as I sat on the veranda waiting for a car to take me back to my hotel and wishing I could have chosen a jewel, the prince himself suddenly appeared and threw a tiny package into my lap. 'Have this,' he said, smiling a little, 'I believe it is unlucky.' I undid the parcel and inside was a beautiful opal ring. Opals are supposed to bring bad luck, but happily not for Scorpios — my sign.

Later, the Nizam did something extremely kind for me. Uncle George, the relative we'd stayed with in the Nilgiri Hills when Tessa and I were children, had died; his lawyer in India described his papers as 'fascinating', but no one could think how to get them back to the UK. Then the Nizam, who had yet another palace in the Nilgiri Hills, offered to have a suitcase of them collected and sent to my parents. Actually, it might have been better if he hadn't — when Mum and Dad went through the case it was full of IOUs: old Uncle George seemed to have become a moneylender. But in amongst them were two fat Victorian letters which, looked at very briefly, seemed to be an account by an English woman of her capture, escape, recapture and further escape, from mutineers/ freedom fighters in the Indian Mutiny/First War of Independence. The letters were written and overwritten, and very hard to decipher, so Dad put them to one side and took all the other papers out into the garden to burn on a bonfire. We never knew how it happened, but when we settled down to read the historic letters, they had disappeared — somehow they had been put on to the bonfire too, and gone up in flames. We were devastated; we hadn't read them, we didn't know the story and we

had no idea who they were written by —
had she been our ancestor? It was all gone for
ever.

★   ★   ★

The night before I left my hotel in Hyderabad to
begin my journey back to London, I sorted out
all the stuff I'd been carrying around on my
travels in India and threw the things I no longer
needed into the wastepaper basket, including a
half-empty Tampax box.

I thought no more about this until, just as my
taxi was pulling away from the kerb and into the
traffic to head for the airport, a man came
running out of the hotel waving my Tampax box
— but it was too late, we were already en route.
That wasn't the end of it, though: just after I'd
gone through Departures I heard someone
calling and turned around, and there at the end
of the hall was the man from the hotel still
waving the Tampax box. They wouldn't let me go
back, so I tried to mime that it didn't matter, not
to worry, but he was still sadly waving the box
when I took a last look. As the plane started its
race down the runway, I had a horrible fear that
I might see him running alongside, still waving
the box.

The fashion shoot we'd done in India went
into the magazine, and a short piece by John
about the old Nizam's purchases, still in their
boxes from the Army and Navy Stores, did too
(photographs by Tony), but Dennis never used
our Nizam piece in *Nova*, I am not sure why. I

think perhaps he felt it was a bit remote and meaningless to our readers, and he was probably right, but I am glad I had the adventure.

# 18

One of the stories I was responsible for at *Nova* was Nostradamus. At that time very few people, apart from some academics, had heard of the medieval seer, but I went to a dinner party and met a young woman Erika Cheetham, who had studied him at university, and she had me spellbound all evening with stories about his prophecies. I rushed into *Nova* next day to tell Dennis about it, and asked if we could commission Erika to write a piece about him. 'If he is so darned clever,' said Dennis, 'why can't he write the piece himself?' (I had forgotten to mention that Nostradamus had lived 450 years before.) I thought this was so funny that I told the story to *Private Eye* at one of their lunches — I was always so grateful to be invited that I felt I had to pay my way somehow — and they put it in the magazine. Dennis was furious and was about to fire someone he suspected of the leak, so I had to step forward and admit it was me — which I found hard, because you never wanted Dennis to think badly of you. He forgave me because I'd confessed. Once I was leaning over Dennis's desk, going through the typescript of a piece I had done, when he suddenly turned and said, 'If you think that's the way to get your work published you are very much mistaken.' I didn't know what he was talking about but then I looked down and realised my blouse was half undone, revealing my cleavage — I was utterly mortified to think that Dennis might imagine I'd done it on purpose, and rushed to button it up again.

In the spring of 1970 Brigitte Bardot, our early-Sixties idol, whose hair and clothes we copied so enthusiastically, was thirty-five. THIRTY-FIVE! It seemed so *old*. I thought it would be a great coup if I could interview her for the magazine — and it looked as if I had struck lucky when I found a photographer friend of hers, Ghislain Dussart, who said he would approach her on our behalf. She agreed, as long as the photograph was taken by him, and so I went to Paris to talk to her, but at the last minute, in the studio, she decided she did not want to meet me face to face, and I had to write out my questions — which were passed to her in the next room, where she wrote the replies. 'Who does your hair?' was one of my queries. 'My right hand,' she responded. There were several pages of my questions and her slightly flip answers and I took them back to London and used them to write my piece, after which they disappeared from my desk: someone obviously thought they might be worth something one day. I was upset because they were such a wonderful souvenir of the great star.

We worked hard at *Nova* — I am astonished when I look back through my old copies to see how many pieces I did each month and how elaborate they often were. A feature about networks had seven photographs with between five to fifteen people in each one: my subject had a 'family' network, a 'work' network, a 'riding' network, a 'young-mums' network, an 'army-wives' network and so on, and we photographed them all. It must have taken days to set that lot up. The other thing that amazes me when I flip through the old mags is the number of man-made fibres being advertised — page after page of Crimplene, Terylene, Orlon, Trevira, Celon, Tricel, Terlenka, Courtelle, Ban-Lon, Dacron and Bri-Nylon (they made terrible sheets out of this that produced shock-giving static). Do these all still exist? I wonder.

★ ★ ★

I was fortunate to share an office with a man I liked as much as Dennis: David Jenkins. While I was doing frivolous pieces like revamping the Queen, David was covering serious social and political stories. Something he wrote upset the head of IPC, our uber-boss Hugh Cudlipp, and David was summoned to a meeting with him. As he set off rather nervously for the appointment he said, 'I'm just off to chew the fat with Cudlipp — or . . . ' he paused ' . . . should I say I am off to chew the cud with Fatlipp?' Whenever I remember this it makes me laugh out loud.

For some crazy reason David was determined to celebrate his thirtieth birthday in Ouaga-dougou in West Africa — he did, at a restaurant called L'Eau Vive, run by nuns. He never came back to British journalism, ending up, many adventures and two books later, in Japan, with a Japanese wife and daughter, translating haikus.

He died much too young, in 2000. I miss him still.

★ ★ ★

In March 1968, three months after Tessa and I returned from our adventures in the East, the famous anti-Vietnam War rally took place in London. Tessa and I, already veteran marchers, and now with our first-hand experience of the war, obviously had to go. Somehow — he must have been in my sister Moira's office when I visited her at the *Sunday Times* one day (as I did very often) — I found myself chatting to Fabian of the Yard, the famous detective who was now retired and working as head of security at the paper. I told him we were planning to march and he said, 'You'll have to watch yourselves, girl. My sources tell me that the American Embassy will open fire on protesters rather than let them storm the building; be very careful.'

Tessa and I joined the rally in Trafalgar Square where everything was good-humoured, but when we got to Park Lane the huge Maoist group decided to go for the American Embassy and branched away towards Grosvenor Square. With Fabian's words in our minds, Tessa and I tried to get out of the crowd, but instead found ourselves swept along and finally pushed against a wall of policemen who had formed a barrier across the street to try and prevent anyone getting near the square; I remember us trying to tell the policeman we were crushed against that we were casual bystanders, not Maoist troublemakers. Protesters were throwing marbles and firecrackers under the police horses' hoofs, it was becoming ugly and violent, and even more so when the police cordon broke and the Maoist crowd surged forward down the street towards the embassy, but in the chaos we managed to fight our way out and escape. (The Maoists did reach the square and the embassy; lots of people got hurt and lots more arrested, but no one got shot by the Americans.)

★   ★   ★

One of my best friends at that time was Felicity, a kindred spirit, funny and kind, who worked in public relations, made dangly hippy necklaces (I still have one) and was married to the star newsreader of the day, Reginald Bosanquet. Somehow, towards the end of that year, they contrived to get me the job of fashion reporter on the ITV *News at Ten* (which was quite a new programme then). I didn't have to do a huge number of stories for them, so it didn't clash with my job on *Nova*, and I had lots of ideas for the programme, but I was hopelessly nervous and everything I did involved dozens of 'takes': 'Here I am in the House of Dior . . . oh sorry, can we do that again'; 'Here I am . . . oh sorry'; 'Here I am at the House of Dior, in only a matter of hours we will know what women will be wearing next winter . . . oh sorry', and so on. Every scene had to be filmed about ten times. The only thing that made it bearable was that my cameraman was so patient and kind. Once, I thought it would be interesting to interview the famous Sixties designer Ossie Clark, but this became a different kind of nightmare because the only response I could get to any question was a grunted 'Yeah', so I ended up babbling away, the only one of us doing any talking: 'Ossie, do you see women dressing in a more feminine way this summer or do you think the idea of trousers is going to catch on and stay popular?' 'Yeah.'

Even now, all these years later, my stomach does a little lurch when I hear that dramatic music that introduces *News at Ten*.

The one thing I was really proud of there was a very short film we made about all the different fashions being worn by ordinary women in the streets — hot-pants, miniskirts, long skirts, hippy clothes, trouser suits, etc. The background music we chose was 'Melting Pot' by Blue Mink ('what we need is a great big melting pot'); the film was unusual for ITN and made an appropriate finale to that most exciting decade when it was shown as the last item on the news, on the last night of the Sixties.

★ ★ ★

Reggie Bosanquet was renowned for his drinking which gave him a flushed complexion; this hadn't really mattered as everything had always been in black and white, but when colour came to ITV in 1969 (the year I worked for *News at Ten*) I heard two girls from the make-up department talking in the ladies' room. 'What are we going to do about Reggie?' one asked. 'What do you mean?' responded the other. 'Well, he is *purple*, isn't he. What are we going to do about that?'

★  ★  ★

Dennis left the magazine, David went to Africa, new people came and the *Nova* I loved began to turn into something else, so when I was offered a job as women's editor on the *Observer*, I accepted it. Moira, who was by then the distinguished women's editor of *The Times*, was a much more suitable candidate for the *Observer*, and we joked together that it was all a mistake and that they had approached the wrong sister. (Which, since I was sacked a year and a bit later, was probably true, but I never managed to get them to confess to it: when I left, I asked the editor why he had hired me; he said it was because he hadn't felt very well that day.)

In the meantime, what none of us close to her knew was that Moira had found a small lump in her breast which, over the months, had grown from peanut- to walnut-size. Cancer was a taboo subject: she had no idea that there was any treatment available so she'd kept all this to herself and worried alone — until one day, looking through a magazine in the hairdresser's, she saw a small advertisement for bras made for women who had had mastectomies. She had never heard the word before but quickly found out what it meant — and went straight to the

239

doctor. Moira was probably the first person to write openly and honestly about breast cancer and about her own mastectomy and primitive radiotherapy treatment (there was no chemotherapy at that time); until then everyone had shied away from any mention of 'breasts' or 'cancer'. Moira changed all that.

\* \* \*

Just as I joined the *Observer* I met AW, but cruelly, only a couple of weeks later, he was obliged to take up a posting in Nepal and our relationship had to continue by letter for the next year (there were no emails in those days of course). Looking back now, perhaps that was the best way for us to get to know each other: you can be more direct in a letter somehow.

By this time — the beginning of the Seventies — there was a lot of public debate going on about whether Britain should or should not join the Common Market, as the EU was known then; all very similar to the current argument about whether we should *stay* in it. A national referendum was planned, but long before it was to take place there were posters and advertisements urging people to say YES or NO to the idea. In the meantime I myself was in a bit of a dither about whether to marry AW or not (he hadn't actually asked me as yet, but I suspected he would). I must at some stage have poured out my heart to the fatherly printers at the *Observer*, because just as I was given my notice and preparing to leave the paper, they presented me with my very own personalised poster which said BRIGID KEENAN SAYS YES TO AW. So when he did finally propose, I took their advice, and lived happily ever after.

# Epilogue

Moira died in 1972, leaving us all desolate (as well as her many readers who looked on her as a friend). She was only thirty-nine years old and left two young boys and her husband who, luckily, are still with us. Her eldest granddaughter (there are three) looks exactly like her — she had a baby girl in 2014 so Moira became a great-grandmother, she would have been thrilled.

Tessa moved with her husband and son up to Scotland and then to Cumbria — I felt more and more thankful to have AW.

My brother David had a wonderful big family of six; he became Adjutant General of the British Army and was knighted.

Mum and Dad lived to a great old age — Dad to over ninety, Mum to eighty-eight. Mum became anxious and worried about things as she grew older and we christened her Doomwatch. I asked her once why she always expected the worst and she said, 'Because in my experience that is what usually happens,' and when I think of her life — widowed with a newborn baby at twenty-one, her brother disappearing in the Spanish Civil War, Moira dying of cancer so young; not to mention all the many heartbreaking partings through the years, plus the major displacement of moving back to England in middle age — I can see what she meant.

No one knew what happened to Uncle Dick

for decades — the family all hoped he was in prison in Spain and would be released one day. My mother and aunt sometimes thought they spotted him in a crowd on TV, or in the background of a newspaper picture. There was no closure in their lifetimes, but not long ago an extraordinary thing happened: my cousin Simon picked up a free newspaper on a train, and in it — incredibly — was a letter asking for relatives of Dick Moss to get in touch. It was from a researcher looking into the men who had volunteered to fight in the International Brigades, and through him Simon learned that Dick had been killed by machine-gun fire very soon after his arrival in Spain, along with a colleague, Walter Caspers. Their deaths were witnessed by a fellow-fighter called Harold Collins. In 2006 a mosaic commemorating the volunteers, including Dick, was unveiled on the embankment wall under the Westway flyover next to Portobello Road.

Joan, our young aunt who married the Dutchman, had three children — which meant more, younger cousins to have fun with (they all loved dressing up as much as we did). Sadly she died when she was only fifty-three; we are close to her offspring.

The cousins my sisters and I grew up with — Jinny, Prue and Simon — all have families and grandchildren now; once in a blue moon we have a reunion.

I hope they recognise this account of our shared childhood — they may not, of course, because we all remember things in different ways. I have already come across this: when I finished *Full Marks for Trying* I rather timidly told Prue that I had written a memoir about the fun we had together with her and her family when we were children, and she said, 'How strange, I have written a memoir too, and you and Tessa hardly come into it at all.' I should not have been surprised — she and Jinny were older than us and away at boarding school a lot of the time; we younger ones must have hardly entered their thoughts.

I am aware that I have been incredibly lucky in so many ways — with the unexpected chances I have had, with my family, with the friends I grew up with — and the ones I have made over the years, with fellow journalists in Vietnam, with my work colleagues at Westminster Press, the *Daily Express*, the *Sunday Times, Nova, News at Ten* and the *Observer*. I'd like to mention the printers Mr Davy and Mr Darker who protected me like guardian angels — magically condensing or expanding my pieces to fit the available space and generally advising me on life. I thank them all, and I thank David Godwin my agent, and everyone at Bloomsbury, especially my other guardian angel and dearly loved editor, Alexandra Pringle.

The story of AW and my lives together is told in *Diplomatic Baggage* and *Packing Up*.